CW01082473

The
Great Siege
of
Newcastle
1644

The Great Siege of Newcastle 1644

of

ROSIE SERDIVILLE AND JOHN SADLER

Dedicated to all Time Bandits, past and present

Cry, valiant soldiers, laid not your arms,
Listen to the whispers of the night.
Look into your heart and seek,
Find the truth and fight.
Let not your courage be meek.
Like the lion roar.
Worthy your part play, comrades, when battle has begun,
Loosen the dogs of war.
Death shall be your only song,
And like the brave, shall leave their mark in a lonely grave.

Jennifer Laidler

First published 2011

The History Press
The Mill, Brimscombe Port
Stroud, Gloucestershire, GL5 2QG
www.thehistorypress.co.uk

© Rosie Serdiville and John Sadler, 2011

The right of Rosie Serdiville and John Sadler to be identified as the
Authors of this work has been asserted in accordance with the
Copyrights, Designs and Patents Act 1988.

All rights reserved. No part of this book may be reprinted
or reproduced or utilised in any form or by any electronic,
mechanical or other means, now known or hereafter invented,
including photocopying and recording, or in any information
storage or retrieval system, without the permission in writing
from the Publishers.

British Library Cataloguing in Publication Data.
A catalogue record for this book is available from the British Library.

ISBN 978 0 7524 5989 9

Typesetting and origination by The History Press
Printed in Great Britain

Contents

Preface

As a boy, youth and young man, one of the co-authors spent many hours inside Newcastle Keep, that great dark tower so anachronistically placed, surrounded by the rush and consequence of a much later and dismissive era. It has withstood several centuries of Scottish raiders, their Tudor reiver descendants, the ravaging of civil wars, a brash Industrial Revolution and the neglect of contemptuous progress. Relatively few medieval citadels survive in our major cities, the White Tower of London being almost certainly the grandest.

Newcastle's keep was already old when King Charles I raised his standard at Nottingham in that distant summer of 1642, thereby igniting a conflict that would rage and then splutter for another eighteen years till, after a vast effusion of blood and treasure, his son ascended a throne vacant since the regicide of 1649. It would be reasonable to assert that none of those who embarked upon the course of civil strife intended, at that point, to kill the King and establish a republic. Their aims were far more conservative and the vast majority of Parliamentarians would have recoiled from being tarred by any revolutionary brush. It was intended that the royal prerogative be curtailed, rather than cut off. None who marched in the early days behind Parliament's banner had any notion of redistributing wealth. The wars were fought more for control than for radical change. Many would be astonished by the changes strife engendered, less than happy with the consequences and the rise of radical sectaries. Many would be surprised by their own actions – few of the regicides, for example, would have ever contemplated at the outset that they might feel themselves finally driven down such a path. We should not lose sight of the fact that, considering the size of our population in the mid-seventeenth century, the Civil Wars took, pro rata, a worse toll than even the First World War.

The Great Siege and Storming of Newcastle in the autumn of 1644 was an important episode in significant period during the First Civil War (1642–46) and yet it is one which is largely forgotten. This modern study of the siege seeks to shed light upon the nature of polity and division within urban communities and how local factors influenced and shaped allegiances. In the case of Newcastle this led to a tragic and ultimately futile campaign that could have only one outcome. It is said that the term 'Geordies' was coined during a later conflict, the 1715 Jacobite Rebellion, when the Newcastle miners and artisans were so universally Whig in sentiment they drowned out calls for 'King James' with cheers for King George or Geordie. This appears a fundamental shift from the position some sixty years earlier when the city was so resolutely held for the exiled Stuart's father. Yet the situation on Tyneside during the Civil Wars was by no means as clear cut or so demonstrably partisan as might, at first glance, appear to be the case.

The late Professor Terry, who published a series of erudite papers in *Archaeologia Aeliana* in the closing years of the nineteenth century and was a distinguished scholar who had done much work on the army of the Covenanters, provided a detailed study of the primary source material. An interesting local work had earlier been complied in 1889 and subsequently reprinted in 1932 under the title *The Siege and Storming of Newcastle*. Most of the recent writers on the military aspects of the Civil Wars have neglected both the winter campaign in the north east during those early snowbound months of 1644 and the subsequent autumn siege and storming. Even Gardiner in his great history, provides us with scant detail. A more recent and local historian, Stuart Reid, who is a constant and accomplished student of the pike and shot era, has written a carefully researched and lucid account of the campaigns of 1644 but does not shed light upon the subsequent siege.

For the enthusiast and collector of battlefields the city holds many traces, some of which still rise unscathed from the post-industrial detritus around. The Civil War tour is more fully discussed in appendix two. This co-author can claim to have had a long association of involvement with the Keep as both father and father-in-law were representatives of the Society of Antiquaries with responsibility for fabric and collections and he spent some school summers in anorak heaven cleaning and displaying arms and armour. Without that, perhaps this history might not have been written.

Acknowledgements

Thanks are due from the authors to Anna Flowers and colleagues from Newcastle City Libraries, Colm O' Brien and other colleagues at the North East Centre For Lifelong Learning, Nicky Clarke and members of the Society of Antiquaries of Newcastle upon Tyne, the staff of the Great North Museum, the Literary and Philosophical Society of Newcastle upon Tyne, Liz Ritson, Jo Raw and staff at Woodhorn County Museum and Archive, Adam Goldwater and Gillian Dean of Tyne and Wear Museums, Bill Griffiths of the Museums Hub, Tony Ball of Newcastle Keep, Robert Cowper, the late Professor George Jobey, the late Alec Bankier, Charles Wesencraft, Dr Jo Bath, Bill and Diane Pickard, Sarah-Jayne Goodfellow, Diane Trevena, Doug Chapman, Tony Hall and Lyn Dodds, to Adam Barr for the photographs, Jennifer Laidler for the verse extracts and Chloe Rodham for the maps; another successful collaboration. For all errors and omissions the authors remain, as ever, responsible.

Quotes from Napoleon's maxims are taken from the late Dr David Chandler's *The Military Maxims of Napoleon* (Greenhill: London, 2002).

All pictures are from the author's collection unless otherwise stated.

Timeline

1625–39

June 1625 – Charles I of England marries Catholic Henrietta Maria, daughter of Henry IV of France

May 1626 – Charles dismisses Parliament

March 1628 – Parliament recalled; issue of the Thirty Nine Articles

7 June 1628 – Petition of Right

22 August 1628 – James Villiers, Duke of Buckingham is murdered

March 1629 – The Three Resolutions; nine MPs arrested

1632 – Thomas Wentworth ('Black Tom Tyrant' & latterly Earl of Strafford) is appointed Lord Deputy of Ireland

August 1633 – William Laud is appointed Archbishop of Canterbury

18 June 1633 – Charles is crowned King of Scotland in Holyrood Palace

1634–6 – Imposition of Ship Money

February 1638 – Attempted imposition of 'Laud's Liturgy'; Scots enter into Solemn League and Covenant

June 1638 – John Hampden tried for refusing to pay Ship Money

1639 – The pacification of Berwick; First Bishops' War ended

1640

13 April – The Short Parliament

28 August – The Rout of Newburn Ford

21 October – Treaty of Ripon

November – The Long Parliament

1641

20 May – Execution of Strafford

Summer – Triennial Act

Late summer – Rebellion in Ireland breaks out

22 October – Catholic revolt in Ireland

November – The Grand Remonstrance

1642

4 January – Attempt to arrest the five members

March – The Militia Ordinance

April – Charles before the gates of Hull

June – The Nineteen Propositions

July – First Siege of Hull

22 August – Charles raises the royal standard at Nottingham; the Civil War begins

23 September – Skipton Castle besieged

23 October – Battle of Edgehill

13 November – Charles halts before the Parliamentarian forces at Turnham Green

1643

27–29 February – Newark attacked by Ballard

13 April – Battle of Ripplefield

18 June – Skirmish at Chalgrove Field (John Hampden killed)

23 June – Battle of Adwalton Moor

13 July – Battle of Roundaway Down

July – Chester besieged

10 August – Gloucester besieged

20 September – First Battle of Newbury

25 September – Scots enter into Solemn League and Covenant

11 October – Battle of Winceby

November – Basing House besieged and relived

29 November – Anglo-Scottish Treaty formalised

25 December – Pontefract besieged by Lord Fairfax

1644

19 January – Scots cross the border into Northumberland

25 January – Battle and relief of Nantwich

28 January – Scots at Morpeth

3 February – Scots storm the Shieldfield Fort

19 February – Skirmish at Corbridge

1 March – Pontefract again besieged

March – The Wearside Campaign

21 March – Prince Rupert relieves Newark

22 April – Marquis of Newcastle besieged in York

10 May – Montrose and the Earl of Crawford launch unsuccessful attack on Morpeth Castle

29 May – Morpeth surrenders to the Royalists

June – Rupert lays siege to and captures Liverpool

25 June – A further Scottish force under Callendar crosses the border

24 July – Battle of Marston Moor

27 July – Scots return north, leaguer of Newcastle begins

August–October – Siege of Newcastle

19 October – Storming of Newcastle

Dramatis Personae

John Belasyse, 1st Baron Belasyse (1615–1689)

The second son of the 1st Viscount Fauconberg, North Riding gentry and staunch Catholic. He joined the King's Oxford army having raised a regiment of horse and taken command of his father's foot regiment. He fought at Edgehill and the First Battle of Newbury before being transferred to Newcastle's army early in 1644, taking control of York when the marquis moved north to confront the Scots. He was left with the unenviable task of containing the resurgent Fairfaxes with slender resources. Having lost Bradford, he was captured in the Parliamentarian assault at Selby on 11 April, remaining a prisoner till January 1645.

William Cavendish, Marquis of Newcastle (1593–1678)

A grandson of the formidable Bess of Hardwick. In his youth, more famed for his equestrian and fencing skills than academic achievement, he was nonetheless a distinguished member of a glittering scientific circle in the 1630s. On the death of his father in 1613 he inherited the Cavendish estates, was created Viscount Mansfield in 1620 and Earl of Newcastle eight year later. He was, on his mother's side, a representative of the old Northumbrian Ogle line. An accomplished courtier who expended vast sums in support of the King, he was governor to the Prince of Wales. No soldier, his service in the Bishops Wars was marked only by his hostility to the Earl of Holland. He raised his famous tercio of Whitecoats to serve Charles in the north, where he was placed in charge of Royalist forces with military advice from a number of experienced captains such as Goring, Langdale and Eythin (*see* p. 13). In June 1642, he was elevated to his Marquisate and defeated the Fairfaxes resoundingly at Adwalton Moor. He fled the realm after Marston Moor only returning with the Restoration.

Sir Hugh Cholmley, 1st Baronet (1600–1657)

Elected as MP for Scarborough in 1624, his regiment fought at Edgehill. Subsequently defected from Parliament's side and was appointed as a local commander by the Earl of Newcastle with responsibility for the northern section of the Yorkshire coast. After the disaster at Marston Moor, he continued to hold Scarborough for the King before surrendering in July 1645. His final years were spent in exile.

Edward Conway, 2nd Viscount Conway, 2nd Viscount Killultagh (1594–1655)

Son of the 1st Viscount. An Oxford scholar, he studied the art of war under the aegis of his uncle by marriage, Sir Horace Vere and served several terms as MP for Warwick. He was moved to Ireland after the debacle at Newburn in 1640.

Sir John Digby, 1st Earl of Bristol (1580–1653)

Scion of Warwickshire gentry and educated at Cambridge, Digby embarked upon a diplomatic career acting as ambassador to Spain from 1611–24. He failed to broker a Spanish alliance and, though raised to his earldom in 1622, fell foul of the King and spent several years as a prisoner before being released through Parliament's intervention. Though he agreed with some aspects of parliamentary reform, he remained a Royalist at heart and was imprisoned by them in turn. He died in exile.

Ferdinando, 2nd Lord Fairfax (1584–1648)

Fairfax, whose seat was at Denton Hall in Wharfedale, has always been rather overshadowed by the achievements of his eldest son Sir Thomas (see below). He did, however, serve a military apprenticeship in the Netherlands before serving Charles I in the First Bishops' War. He was essentially a moderate though opposed to abuses of the Prerogative and remained steadfast in his allegiance to Parliament.

Sir Thomas, 3rd Lord Fairfax (1612–1671)

'Black Tom' was the first Lord General of the New Model Army and led them to decisive victory at Naseby. Upright, chivalrous and honourable, a lion in battle, though somewhat inclined to hypochondria, he was less sure in politics where his moderation became unfashionable, leading to a distance between he and Cromwell. He survived the Restoration and ended his days in quiet seclusion.

Sir Thomas Glemham (1594–1649)

A scion of Suffolk gentry, Glemham served his military apprenticeship in Europe from 1610–17. He served in Buckingham's ill-conceived expedition to La Rochelle then acted as governor of Hull, accompanying Charles I on his abortive attempt to gain control of the city. He next governed York before being sent north in November 1643 to watch the border, falling back before Leven's army in January 1644. After the Sunderland campaign and Newcastle's withdrawal into York he resumed the governorship, remaining proactive during the siege. After Marston Moor was lost he was left with skeleton forces and a hopeless position. Nonetheless, he managed to negotiate remarkably lenient terms. Thereafter he continued to serve the King as governor of Oxford. He died in exile in Holland.

Lord George Goring (1608–1657)

Perhaps the very ideal of the *beau sabreur* – a popular and dashing cavalier. Born of Sussex gentry, he married an Irish heiress in 1629 but squandered most of her cash on drink and dice. He served with some distinction in the Netherlands and was elected MP for Portsmouth. Regarded as a Parliamentarian, he was given responsibility for the defence of the city but declared for the King once the standard had been raised. He defeated Fairfax at Seacroft Moor but was subsequently captured and held in the Tower until being exchanged in spring 1644. He was able to join Rupert in time to fight well and with all his customary dash at Marston Moor. His career then entered a downward spiral and he died, penniless in Madrid at the age of forty-nine.

James Graham, Marquis of Montrose (1612–1650)

Montrose is one of the most renowned and quixotic figures of the Civil Wars. He inherited his lands and title from his father on the latter's death in 1626. An advocate of the Covenant, he served the Estates well until his allegiance to the King proved too strong. Disregarded by Rupert he nonetheless went on to campaign successfully in Scotland during the 'Year of Miracles'. This came to an abrupt and bloody finale when he was defeated by David Leslie at Philliphaugh. He never regained his former glory and died an ignominious death at the vengeful hands of his former allies. His legend, however, persists.

James King, Lord Eythin (1589–1652)

An Orcadian by birth, King was a natural grandson of James V. He learned his trade under Gustavus and then Leslie where he served with some merit. He was never in step with the Covenanters, leaning towards the King. He served Newcastle as a competent chief of staff though, after January 1644 and Leslie's invasion, he was treated with some suspicion. This festered at York where his marked antipathy to Rupert proved damaging. He died in exile in Sweden.

Sir Marmaduke Langdale (1598–1661)

Born in Beverley, Langdale fought in the Palatinate, receiving his knighthood in 1628. A leading member of the Yorkshire gentry, he opposed the Ship Tax but was still trusted by the King and created Lord-Lieutenant of the shire in 1639. A loyal cavalier, he retained command of Newcastle's cavalry units after Marston Moor. Brigaded as the Northern Horse, they noted for their dash and fire if not for their discipline.

Alexander Leslie, Earl of Leven (1580–1661)

Despite being illegitimate, Leslie pursued an active military career from an early age, serving in the Dutch Wars and then with great distinction under Gustavus. He fought at Lutzen in 1632, where his patron was killed. Despite this, he continued to serve under Queen Christina and remained until 1636, when he retired as a full field marshall. On returning to Scotland, and regarded as the nation's leading soldier, he was the natural choice to command the Covenanter army. In the Second Bishops' War he showed masterly skill in routing the King's forces at Newburn Ford and taking Newcastle. He returned at the head of the army in January 1644 and had conduct of the campaign in the north. He commanded all Parliamentarian forces at Marston Moor but then and thereafter he failed to display his former energy, clearly suffering from the rigours of campaigning. He went on to command Parliament's forces during the siege and storming of Newcastle.

David Leslie, 1st Newark (1600–1682)

The son of the 1st Earl of Lindores, he was the nephew of the Earl of Leven. Leslie learned his profession in the Swedish service and acted as Leven's second in command in 1644. His cavalry did good service at Marston Moor and it was he who finally cornered and defeated Montrose at Philiphaugh, though the victory was soured by atrocity. He fought for Charles II after 1650 and hemmed Cromwell into the Port at Dunbar. Interference from covenanting clergy affected his ability to command and provided an opportunity for Cromwell to strike and win what was perhaps his greatest victory.

John Lilburne (1613?–1657)

Known as 'Freeborn John', Lilburne was a native of Bishop Auckland who attended Newcastle's Royal Grammar School. He became a celebrated agitator and pamphleteer. Flogged and imprisoned by the King, he fought with some distinction for Parliament at Edgehill, was subsequently captured and exchanged, next serving with the Eastern Association. He was an intimate of Cromwell's, though no favourite of Manchester who considered him a dangerous lunatic. His libertarian and Leveller view put him at odds with Cromwell after the Putney Debates and most of his later years were spent in gaol though he was increasingly paroled as his religious views softened and he became a Quaker. He died of fever probably at the age of forty-two.

James Livingston, Lord Almond & 1st Earl of Callendar (d.1674)

The third son of the 1st Earl of Linlithgow, Livingston learnt his trade in the Dutch Wars but never learned to love the covenant. He served Leslie as chief-of-staff in the Second Bishops' War but sided later with Montrose and signed the Cumbernauld Bond. He was reconciled to the King in 1641, but despite doubts over his loyalties served Leslie again after the latter led the army into England in 1644. He remained in charge of reserves stationed on the border till marching south in June. There were mutterings over his alleged reluctance to fight against Montrose but he served his commanding general throughout the blockade, siege and storming of Newcastle.

Sir John Marley (1590–1672)

A staunch and unrepentant Royalist, Marley famously defended Newcastle as mayor in 1644. His uncompromising stand seems to have earned the resentment not just of the Scots but also of many less committed townsfolk. He escaped from custody (or was allowed to escape) into exile but may have returned as early as 1658 to facilitate the Restoration. He again served as mayor in 1661.

Sir Henry Slingsby (1602–1658)

A Yorkshire landowner and West Riding MP, related by marriage to Belasyse, he fought in the Bishops' Wars and officered the queen's escort from Bridlington. He fought for the King at both Marston Moor and Naseby, remaining a convinced Royalist. He plotted to overthrow Cromwell and was involved in a scheme to seize Hull. When this was uncovered he was tried and subsequently executed.

Henry Wilmot, 1st Earl of Rochester (1612–1658)

A constant and successful Royalist, Wilmot learned the art of war in Holland, where he served with Goring. After service in the Bishops' Wars he pursued a distinguished career as a Royalist officer, participating in many actions, beginning with Powicke Bridge though he could not get along with Prince Rupert. His finest hour was victory over Waller and the virtual destruction of Parliament's western forces at Roundway Down. His later career was controversial but always colourful. He died of fever at Sluys in Flanders.

Sir Henry Vane (1589–1655)

A Kentishman by birth, Vane qualified at the Bar and was knighted by James I. Able and ambitious, he bribed his way into a string of political offices, rising to high favour with Charles I, who entrusted him with a series of high-level diplomatic missions. He subsequently quarrelled with Strafford and was a prosecution witness at the latter's trial. After the setback of the Second Bishops' War, he retained the King's confidence but subsequently fell from grace and defected to Parliament. His accumulation of wealth in the 1630s had enabled him to acquire Raby, Barnard Castle and Long Newton in Durham. He remained high in Parliament's counsels though no friend to Lilburne and the Levellers. There was a suggestion that his death was suicide.

Glossary

Abatis – Improvised defences of cut branches planted points outwards toward an enemy, sixteenth-century barbed wire

Ambuscade – Trap or ambush

Backsword – A form of weapon with one sharpened cutting edge and the other flattened and blunt, primarily a horseman's weapon designed for the cut

Banquette – Earth step within the parapet which allows the defenders to fire

Barbican – A form out defended outer gateway designed to shield the actual gate itself

Bartizan – A small corner turret projecting over the walls

Bastion – Projection from the curtain wall of a fort, usually at intersections, to provide a wider firing platform and to allow defenders to enfilade (flanking fire) a section of the curtain

Batter – Outward slope at the base of a masonry wall to add strength and frustrate mining efforts

Battery – A section of guns, may be mobile field artillery or a fixed defensive position within a defensive circuit

Blinde(s) – A bundle of brushwood or planks used to afford cover to trenches

Brattice – A temporary series of timber hoardings affording extra cover for defenders

Breast and back – Body armour comprising a front and rear plate section

Breastwork – Defensive wall

Broadsword – A double-edged blade intended for cut or thrust, becoming old-fashioned though many would do service, often with an enclosed or basket hilt

Buff Coat – A leather coat, long skirted and frequently with sleeves, fashioned from thick but pliant hide, replaced body armour for the cavalry

Caliver – A lighter form of musket, with greater barrel length than the cavalry carbine (see below)

Cannon – Heavy gun throwing a 47lb ball; a demi-cannon fired 27lb ball; cannon-royal shot a massive 63lb ball

Caracole – A form of cavalry tactic whereby the riders approach the enemy infantry in ranks, discharging pistols then wheeling aside before contact

Carbine – A short barrelled musket used primarily by cavalry

Case-shot – Also referred to as canister this was a cylindrical shell case, usually tin, sealed in beeswax and caulked with wooden disks, wherein a quantity of balls were packed and filled with sawdust. A cartridge bag of powder was attached to the rear and, on firing, the missile had the effect of a massive shotgun cartridge, very nasty

Casement – A bomb-proof chamber or vault within the defences

Chevaux-de-frise – A large baulk of timber set with sharpened blades to form an improvised defence, often employed to seal or attempt to seal a breach in the defender's walls

Clubmen – Bodies of local men who formed associations of militia to defend their localities against incursions by forces from either of the warring factions – armed neutrals

Commission of Array – This was the ancient royal summons issued through the lords-lieutenants of the counties to raise militia forces, in the context of a civil war such an expedient was of dubious legality as it was clearly unsanctioned by Parliament

Committee of Both Kingdoms – This was brought into being as a consequence of two parliamentary measures (16 February and 22 May 1644) to ensure close cooperation between the English and Scots, Cromwell, Manchester and Essex were all members of the Committee which sat at Derby House

Cornet – A pennant or standard and thus also the junior officer who carried it

Corselet – This refers to a pikeman's typical harness of breast and back, with tassets for the thighs

Counterscarp – Outer slope or wall of a defenders' external ditch or moat

Covered Way (or *Covert*) – A covered or protected position, usually a lowered earth parapet on the counterscarp of an outer glacis

Cuirassier – These were heavy cavalry wearing three-quarter harness, something of an anachronism. Sir Arthur Hesilrige's 'Lobsters' were the most famous example; as the wars progressed reliance upon armour decreased considerably

Culverin – A gun throwing a 15lb ball. Mainly used in siege operations, the guns weighed an average of 4,000lb the lighter demi-culverin threw a 9lb ball and weighed some 3,600lb

Dagg(s) – Wheel-lock horseman's pistols, usually carried in saddle holsters

Dragoon – Essentially mounted infantry, the name is likely derived from 'dragon' a form of carbine; their roles was to act as scouts and skirmishers and they could fight either mounted (rare) or dismounted

Defilade – Where one party, probably a defender, uses any natural or man-made obstacle to shield or conceal their position (see also *enfilade* below)

Drake or *Saker* – Gun firing a 5¼lb ball

Enceinte – The circuit or whole of the defensive works

Enfilade – Where one party is in a position to direct fire onto the longest exposed axis of the other's position, e.g. an attacker is able to shoot along a defender's trench from the flank

Ensign (or *Ancient*) – A junior commissioned officer of infantry who bears the flag from which the name derives

Falcon – Light gun firing a 2¼lb ball

Falconet – Light gun throwing a 1¼lb shot

Field-works – A system of improvised temporary defensive works employed by an army on the march or protecting an encampment

Fleche – A projecting V-shaped defensive outwork

Flintlock or *firelock* – A more sophisticated ignition mechanism than match; the flint was held in a set of jaws, the cock, when released by the trigger, struck sparks from the steel frizzen and showered these into the pan which ignited the main charge

Foot – Infantry

Free Quarter – Troops paying for food and lodgings by a ticket system, requisitioning or outright theft in practice

Fusil – This was a form of light musket usually carried by gunners and latterly by officers, hence 'fusilier'

Gabion – Wicker baskets filled with earth which formed handy building blocks for temporary works or sealing off a breach

Glacis – A sloped earthwork out from the covered way to provide for grazing fire from the curtain

Granado – Mortar shell

Guns – Artillery

Halberd – A polearm, outdated in war but carried as a staff of rank by NCOs

Harquesbusier – An archaic term describing the cavalryman armed with carbine, sword and brace of pistols, the latter sometimes still referred to as 'daggs'

Horse – Cavalry

Linstock – A staff with a forked end to hold match – used for discharging cannon

Lunette – Flanking walls added to a small redan (see below) to provide additional flanking protection and improved fire position; a 'demi-lune' is a crescent or half moon structure built projecting from the curtain to afford greater protection

Magazine – Bomb-proof vault where powder and shot are stored

Main Gauche – Literally 'left hand'; this was a form of dagger used in conjunction with the rapier

Matchlock – The standard infantry firearm, slow and cumbersome, prone to malfunction in wet or wind, it was nevertheless generally reliable. When the trigger was released the jaws lowered a length of lit cord 'match' into the exposed and primed pan which flashed through to the main charge, where the charge failed to ignite this was referred to a 'a flash in the pan'

Matross – A gunner's mate, doubled as a form of *ad hoc* infantry to protect the guns whilst on the march

Meutriere – Or 'murder-hole', a space between the curtain and corbelled out battlements enabling defenders to drop a variety of unpleasant things onto attackers at the base of the wall

Minion – Gun shooting a 4lb ball

Morion – Infantry protective headgear, the morion was a conical helmet with curving protective brim and central ridged comb intended to deflect a downwards cut

Musket – The term refers to any smooth-bored firearm, regardless of the form of lock, rifled barrels were extremely rare, though not unknown at this time

Ordnance – Artillery

Pike – A polearm with a shaft likely to be between 12 and 18ft in length, finished with a diamond-shaped head (see appendix 1)

Postern (Sally Port) – A small gateway set into the curtain allowing re-supply and deployment of defenders in localised attacks on besiegers

Rapier – A slender, long-bladed thrusting weapon, more likely to be owned by gentry; bespoke and more costly than a trooper's backsword

Shot – Musketeers

Ravelin – A large, V-shaped outwork, beyond the ditch or moat, intended to add protection to a particularly vulnerable point

Redan – Smaller than the ravelin, this is a small outwork with two walls set at a salient angle facing the enemy, typically the rear or gorge is uncovered, similar to a fleche

Redboubt – A detached, square, polygonal or hexagonal earthwork or blockhouse

Robinet – Light field gun firing a 1¼lb shot

Scarp – Inner wall of ditch or moat

Sconce – A small detached fort with projecting corner bastions

Snap – Cold rations carried in a 'snapsack'

Swine-Feather – Also known as Swedish feathers, a form of metal-shod stake that could be utilised to form an improvised barrier against an enemy

Tasset – A section of plate armour hinged from the breastplate intended to afford protection to the upper thigh

Tercio – A Spanish term for the military formation, derived from the Swiss model which dominated Renaissance warfare, developed into a more linear formation after the reforms of the Swede Gustavus Adolphus

Terreplein – A level space upon which defenders guns are mounted

Touch-hole – The small diameter hole drilled through the top section of a gun barrel through which the linstock ignites the charge, fine powder was poured in a quill inserted into the touch-hole

Train – A column of guns on the move, the army marches accompanied or followed by the train

Trained Bands – Local militia

Wheel-lock – More reliable and much more expensive than match, this relied upon a circular metal spinning wheel wound up like a clock by key. When the trigger was released the wheel spun and the jaws lowered into contact and fitted with pyrites, showered sparks into the pan

I

Being Introductory

The Forward Youth that would appear
Must now forsake his muses dear,
Nor in the shadows sing
His number languishing

Tis time to leave the books in dust,
And oil the unused armour's rust,
Removing from the wall
The corslet from the hall.

'An Horatian Ode upon Cromwell's return from Ireland' Andrew Marvell (1621–1678)

The first consideration with a general who offers battle should be the glory and honour of his arms; the safety and preservation of his men is only the second; but it is in the enterprise and courage resulting from the former that the latter will most assuredly be found.

Napoleon Bonaparte

Into the Breach

On the afternoon of 19 October 1644, a grey day of autumn, smoke eddied over the scorched walls of the northern city and the jumble of close-packed buildings gapped and scarred by shell. Civil strife, unseen in England since Bosworth and Stoke Fields more than a century and a half ago, was now enjoying a full, bitter flowering. In part this was an ancient grudge, Scots and Northern English, honed by three full centuries of bitter hate and constant strife, from snarling lancers with border names, to crack of cannon and the clothyard storm on a dozen bloodied fields and more.

The attackers shuffled out into columns, a drab legion in ragged hodden grey, morion and corselets scoured to a dull glow. Dry-mouthed, each man stood, waiting, while dour ministers moved along the columns offering the solace of God's word.

Above, the cannonade reached a fury. Great black clouds of sulphurous fumes obscured the lines already half hidden by camp followers burning rubbish, the ancient Scots' smoke screen. Trumpets blared and the assault started, men stumbling forward hefting the ungainly weight of puissant pike or blowing on match, officers drew swords.

It was begun.

The Great Cause

James VI of Scotland and I of England has generally not enjoyed a good press: slack-jawed and unprepossessing, learned yet often foolish, his achievements have been largely overlooked. A proficient linguist who rode and hunted well, he managed to prevail against both the rampant anarchy of the nobility and the arrogant intolerance of the Kirk whilst successfully merging the crowns, no mean task in itself. He is regarded as a highly successful King of Scots. Nonetheless, his English subjects were disappointed: he appeared a poor successor to Elizabeth and his son Charles was even worse. Whilst James, a wily tactician, readily exploited the differences between his opponents, Charles very early mastered the knack of uniting the opposition against him. Charles had many virtues – he was tolerant in an age of creeping intolerance, cultured, pious and brave – yet he showed little interest in his northern kingdom and less understanding. His policy, such as it was, encouraged Laudian-style episcopacy (rule of the Church by bishops), an anathema to many Scots. He excluded the Lords of Session from the Privy Council and then terrified the Scots nobles by threatening to seek recovery of all property taken over since the accession of his grandmother, Mary, in 1542.

These concerns were rendered trivial when Charles thought to introduce the *Book of Canons* (incorrectly labelled as 'Laud's Liturgy', and generally considered more popish than the *English Prayer Book*). Riots ensued and an outraged populace flocked to sign the National Covenant in 1638. As opposition swelled, protestors demanded the withdrawal of the liturgy and the expulsion of the bishops from the Privy Council. Anti-Episcopalian sentiment began to mount. The Covenanters, as the signatories to the Deed were known, sought a free Parliament, the General Assembly of the following year openly defying the King and purporting to abolish episcopacy.

Charles was persuaded to use force against his Scottish subjects, but his attempts to raise a viable army foundered. The rabble he managed to gather drank and pillaged their way north but never amounted to a military expedition. The following year saw Charles once again trying to recruit adequate forces; to no one's surprise, other than perhaps his own, meeting with scant success. The Scots fared better, their regiments swelled and drilled whilst the tide of change gathered momentum. The clerical estate was abolished. The Covenant became an obligation rather than a choice. The executive power rested in a Committee of the Three Estates and the Kirk (the dominant reformed church in Scotland) ably championed by Argyll, took effective control.

Allegedly at the head of 20,000 foot with 2,500 horse★, Alexander Leslie, who had won renown as the defender of Stralsund in the Thirty Years' War, splashed across the Tweed on 20 August 1640. A scratch Royalist force at Newburn on the Tyne, under Lord Conway, sought to bar his passage south. The English could field no more than 3,500 foot, mainly musketeers and perhaps a couple of thousand horse. A brace of earthwork redoubts commanded the ford (on ground now occupied by Stella Power Station). At dusk on 27 August the two armies faced each other over the placid waters. Leslie made good use of the short summer night, causing his guns to be dragged down to the riverbank where they opened the morning's hostilities with a brisk fire. Under cover of the cannons' roar, a vanguard of Life Guards forced the crossing, precipitating a hasty withdrawal by the English which swiftly dissolved into rout. Even a spirited charge by the cavaliers could not stem the rot and the 'rout of Newburn Ford' was quickly ended (*see* chapter 2). Charles now faced the humiliation of seeing virtually the whole of Northumberland and Durham, including Newcastle, under Scots occupation. He was forced to negotiate from a position of weakness, a stance which further dented his crumbling prestige. The concord agreed at Ripon was formally ratified by the King's Commissioners in 1641 and the Scots marched home, having earned their country some £200,000.

* This figure is open to question and is more fully discussed in Chapter Six.

Coals from Newcastle

The lively seventeenth century writer and traveller Celia Fiennes described Newcastle as 'the fairest and richest Town in England, inferior for wealth and building to no city save London and Bristol'. She was not exaggerating. By the 1630s the city's population was fast approaching that of its commercial rival Bristol, probably around 13,000 by the time of the Hearth Tax Assessment of 1665 (assuming a household of approx 4.5 per hearth plus apprentices and servants present in one third of the mercantile properties)[1]. Newcastle was amongst the four largest towns in the country and one of the wealthiest. The map of 1638 showing the defences also gives us invaluable information on the layout and density of the wards. These extended beyond the walls to the north at New Gate and Pilgrim Street Gate, to the west at West Gate and, most of all, in the east at Sandgate. Not all was boom and prosperity; around 41 per cent of households were defined as being 'in poverty' in 1665[2].

Howell[3] suggests those more affluent wards were clustered in the centre of the town (Castle, Guildhall and Quayside). Poorer wards were pressed against the town's ancient walls in the north-east and north-west, with the exception of Sandgate which, while on the outskirts, hugged the course of the river[4]. Howell further calculates that the eight inner wards were the wealthiest area of the town, although they probably held no more than 18 per cent of the population and that the residents of these areas enjoyed disproportional representation on the town's ruling bodies (Common Council and the Twenty Four).

Langton notes that the guild structure had, in previous centuries, led to 'occupational zoning and social class mixing'. Guild members tended to live close to each other with the workshop and/or warehouse occupying the same plot as the living quarters for master and family; journeymen apprentices and servants would have lived in the upper quarters of the same building. This historic pattern was breaking down as wealthier members of the community, particularly the merchant elite, were developing links with the gentry of the surrounding countryside and buying properties outside the city, thus beginning a process of 'gentrification' by progressive disassociation with the urban sprawl which continued into the twentieth century[5].

Langton's general conclusion is that during this period, those of greater wealth and higher status occupations resided in town centres. He also points out there are considerable problems with using Hearth Tax figures as guides to relative wealth and with analysing towns at the level of ward or parish, rather than street by street. However, his own analysis of the cartographic information tends to support Howell's description of the economic zoning of the city[6]. Merchants were increasingly using their wealth to acquire larger homes in the centre. In Newcastle, a swathe of larger houses existed in the area between Castle and Guildhall, although Hearth Tax records do show some larger houses in other areas (the obvious caveat here is that those records relate to the period after the Civil Wars). Militarily, when it came to defending the city by clearing areas beyond the walls, it was those households in poorer wards who suffered most – the larger properties at the centre of the town belonging to 'hostmen' (coal traders and shippers) and others of equivalent socio-economic status, were not subject to the same measure of enforced expediency.

Howell produces a useful table based on evidence taken from the Hearth Tax Assessment of 1665[7]. The contemporary and partisan William Gray uses topography to convey his political message. He emphasises the traditional and long accepted role of Newcastle in protecting the rest of the kingdom from Scottish incursion, employing poetry, description, cartography and morphology to hammer home his view. Certainly, the city's location so close to the long-disputed frontier and the role it played in controlling that border gave it a most particular importance[8]. By the seventeenth century, with the Scottish threat apparently removed, those great traders of the town had become bankers to the whole region from Tees to Tweed. Money flowed out to lord and landowner from the north. Newcastle provided much needed liquid cash to replace it. Certain, select hostmen acted as bankers on an even greater scale. In 1623, Sir William Selby, part of an affinity of northern merchants which included the Delavals and the Belaysyse, was recorded as lending money to London. Merchants formed a cash rich monopoly based on swelling profits from the burgeoning coal trade. Banking status ensured Newcastle's hostmen were creditors to both landlord and tenant: 'This towne unto this countrye, serves in stead of London: by means whereof the countrye is supplied with money'[9].

An opportunity to invest monies, using the profits of trade and realising a return, has long been seen as one of the drivers of the English revolution: a symptom of the frustration with that level of control exercised by the Crown over the economy and a cause of substantial investment in overseas trade. The latter was perceived as more speculative than investing in domestic schemes; both capital risk and potential return being far greater. During this era no retail banking system existed to facilitate capital being transferred around the country. Goldsmiths were able to offer a rudimentary system of secure deposit and could provide credit notes to be drawn on one of their network in another area but such arrangements were essentially *ad hoc* and informal[10].

The banking role of Newcastle's merchants was almost unique and gave them significant control over debtors as well as an opportunity to generate significant returns for themselves. It also meant that these financiers were in a position to enter into joint ventures with gentry anxious to put their lands to commercial use; relationships that might well be cemented in other ways, ideally by dynastic marriages. Connections between the Anderson, Riddell and Liddell families were cemented at the altar, as subsequently was that between the Blacketts and Delavals.

'King Coal' was not the only significant generator of economic prosperity – the cloth trade, maritime activity, leather working, glass and salt-making (there were salt pans at

South Shields and some at North Shields) all played their part. In terms of cultural life, which clings to the coat tails of economic prosperity, the town was exhibiting levels of sophistication. Chamberlains' accounts record payments to travelling players, poets and entertainers[11]. The urban centre acted as a cultural as well as commercial magnet – many of the Northumbrian gentry had town houses, providing opportunities to boost affinities.

Following the Dissolution and 'privatisation' of the mines fuelling an upsurge in mining activity during the 1580s, the city was able to respond to the diminishing importance of previously crucial economic activity such as the production and processing of wool. Newcastle was in an ideal position to supply cheap fuel; deposits were close to the surface, extracted from easily accessed pits. Coal could then be transported by water to the city for shipping on to London. The 'Grand Lease' (rights to exploit mines in Whickham & Gateshead) had been assigned by Queen Elizabeth I to a consortium of Newcastle merchants. By the turn of the seventeenth century, Newcastle was exporting 150,000 tons per year rising to 300,000 tons to London alone in 1650. The value of the London trade becomes clear when we consider how much was being shipped to the rest of the country, some 200,000 tons. Wrightson, quoting Wrigley, observes: 'the heat provided by burning one ton of coal is equivalent to that attainable from the dry wood yielded by an acre of woodland. In terms of energy production, then, the miners, coal owners and merchants of the north-east had provided England with the equivalent of two million acres of woodland per year'[12].

The trade became an increasingly significant occupation for those deprived of other employment outside the city; the turbulent border which had provided employment of a sort, usually violent and illicit, had ceased to exist as an economic factor in that sense. Between 1565 and 1625 the coal trade increased twelvefold. Newcastle coal owners opined that 5,800 men were employed in the Tyneside coal industry in 1637–8[13]. Those other local industries – cloth, maritime activity, leather working, glass and salt-making – were increasingly dependant on coal as a ready source of fuel.

Local Affinities

Despite the historic antipathy between lowland Scots and Northern English, cross-border networks were far more commonplace than the ancient enmity might suggest. Take the Delavals, for example Leslie's daughter Anne was married to Sir Ralph, son of Robert Delaval[14]. Robert was aged thirty at the time of his father's death. He served as sheriff in 1575, 1583 and 1592 and was knighted on 13 April 1603. On his subsequent demise, on 1 January 1607, his eldest son Sir Ralph succeeded him. Ralph Delaval's younger son, Thomas, left a 'catalogue of the acts' of his father, in which he tells us:

> He was a justice of the peace, of the quorum, in commission of oyer and terminer[15], the custos rotulorum[16], a deputy lieutenant; he had been three times sheriff of Northumberland; he was a commissioner for the Borders, one of the high commissioners of Durham, and was twice called upon to give the King an account of county affairs …

When Sir Ralph died on 24 November 1628, his grandson and heir, Ralph, succeeded to a heavily encumbered estate; the young heir was left with barely £100 per year. He had been educated at Oxford, matriculated at Queen's College 15 June 1638 and was admitted to Lincoln's Inn 28 November 1639. At the age of twenty-four he married Anne, widow of Hugh Fraser, and daughter of Alexander Leslie, 1st Earl of Leven, at St Nicholas' Newcastle, on 2 April 1646. On account of his marriage, Ralph Delaval naturally developed close ties with the Presbyterians and was in favour with the Parliamentarians. In November 1649 he became the first Sheriff of Northumberland under the Commonwealth and was returned MP for Northumberland to Richard Cromwell's Parliament 1659. After the Restoration, he was MP for Northumberland in 1660 but lost his seat in 1661.

He was next elected to the Long Parliament in 1677 and served as MP on three subsequent occasions, March and October 1679 and March 1681. He was highly successful with his coal-mining venture at Hartley and he further boosted local industry when he built a bespoke harbour at Seaton Sluice. He was elevated to his baronetcy on 29 June 1660. The 1st baronet's two eldest sons had died childless during his lifetime therefore, on 29 August 1691, he was succeeded by his third son, Sir Ralph. The 2nd baronet died in 1696, whereupon his personal estate was largely consumed in settling his debts. Seaton Delaval and Hartley passed to his widow under the marriage settlement. His only daughter, Diana, married William, son of Edward Blackett of Newby, Yorkshire, in 1699. His successor to the baronetcy and entailed estate was his younger brother, Sir John Delaval[17].

Blackett is a name long associated with the county of Northumberland, linked to Wallington, Matfen and Wylam. They, the Blackett-Ords of Whitfield and the Blackett-Beaumonts, are all believed to descend from Edward Blackett of Hoppyland in County Durham, born in 1557 and perhaps of yeoman status. Edward's grandson, William, pursued a typical seventeenth-century route to success, moving to Newcastle upon Tyne to take up an apprenticeship. William was indentured to one of the boothman and in 1645 admitted to the Merchant Adventurers Company. He built up a considerable fortune and widespread affinity, and was sheriff and mayor of Newcastle. He was an MP from 1673 when he was named baronet. MP from 1673–1680 and, in 1673, he was created a baronet. He bought the particularly grand town house of Anderson Place (on the site of former ecclesiastical buildings), near the prestigious upper end of Pilgrim Street. The wealth which William amassed and which he passed on to his sons, enabled them to establish country estates, completing the process of gentrification, Edward at Newby in Yorkshire and William at Wallington.

Edward Blackett of Hoppyland had another grandson, Christopher (1612–1675), whose family history followed a different course. In 1685 Christopher's son John (1635–1707) bought two farms in the township of Wylam, forming a modest estate for this branch of the family until the twentieth century. More important, however, was the acquisition of lordship of the manor, which carried with it mineral rights. Without these, Christopher's branch of the family would have been very much the poor relations. As it was, the head of the family augmented his income in a variety of ways and younger sons were largely expected to fend for themselves. Blackett of Wylam papers cover the seventeenth to the twentieth centuries, the bulk being from the nineteenth. Whilst many of them relate to the family's coal-mining activities, there are several thousand items of correspondence which illustrate aspects of the lives of members of the extended family and of life in Wylam[18].

Sir Nicholas Cole, elevated to the baronetcy of Brancepeth in 1610 (one of the earliest figures to be declared a 'delinquent' or arch-Royalist by Parliament) came from a line founded by Nicholas and Thomas, sons of James Cole, a smith from Gateshead. Thomas built up a substantial fortune in bills, bonds and other securities, dying in 1620. Nicholas was the father of Ralph Cole (1625–1704), a gifted amateur artist, and had acted as Sheriff of Newcastle in 1620 then as mayor thirteen years later. In 1636 he acquired Brancepeth. These lands had been forfeited through the attainder of Robert Carr, Earl of Somerset, to whom they had previously been granted by James I. The Crown had earlier attainted the estates of the Earl of Westmorland in consequence of his enthusiastic, if hugely ill-judged, participation in the Rising of the Northern Earls in 1569–1570. For his steadfast loyalty to the Royalist cause Nicholas was imprisoned and fined £4,000. He had married Mary, second daughter of Sir Thomas Liddell, of Ravensworth, and left three sons. The eldest of these was Sir Ralph, who managed to inherit the substantive assets and estates of his predecessors, the greater part of which he expended on art and the patronage of artists[20].

The names of Anderson, Liddell and Riddell were all interrelated. Barbara Anderson was the mother of both Thomas Liddell (famous during the Siege of 1644) and Peter Riddell. Thomas married Isabel Anderson (sister of Sir Henry Anderson). The family were also connected to the Carrs, Mitfords, Lumleys, Chapmans, Dents and Fenwicks; all prominent Tyneside families who provided the city a steady crop of both mayors and sheriffs. The Andersons were prominent members of the Merchant Adventurers[21] and linked to the Collingwoods Gascoignes, Selbys Belasyses, Gurwens, Delavals and Darcies[22].

Born in Auckland, County Durham, Robert Lilburne was an elder brother of the celebrated Leveller agitator John Lilburne ('Freeborn John'). Robert served in the army of the Earl of Essex in 1642–3 before raising a regiment of horse in County Durham which became part of Fairfax's Northern Association. In 1646 'Black Tom' made him colonel of a regiment in the New Model Army, one which gained a reputation for rampant radicalism during the political disputes of 1647. Lilburne remained a committed Baptist and opponent of the Presbyterians, active in the army's political protests against service in Ireland and a spokesman at the Saffron Walden confrontation with the parliamentary commissioners in April 1647. Shortly thereafter he was appointed Governor of Newcastle, where he founded the city's first Baptist congregation. Nonetheless missed the Corkbush Field Mutiny in November 1647 in which his regiment participated.

John Blakiston (*c.* 1603–1649), successful mercer and coal merchant, served as an MP and, tellingly, was one of the regicides, staunchly Puritan and anti-Episcopalian. Born at Sedgefield, County Durham, the third son of Marmaduke Blakiston, Prebendary of York and Durham Cathedral, he married Susan Chamber in 1626. He was a fervent financial supporter of those Puritans who had earlier emigrated to America, though he never left the country. In 1636, he entered into a bitter ideological dispute with Yeldard Alvey, an Arminian vicar in Newcastle, accusing him of heresy. Alvey emerged victorious from the fray, thanks to the support from Archbishop Laud. Blakiston was both fined and excommunicated. He served as member for Newcastle in the Long Parliament where he expressed clearly republican ideas even though he was not able to take up his seat until 1641 due to a contested result. In 1645 he was elected Mayor of Newcastle. Four years later, as a commissioner of the High Court of Justice at the trial of King Charles, he was twelfth of the fifty-nine signatories on the death warrant. He died in June 1649. Following the Restoration, his estates were confiscated by the Sheriff of Durham[23].

Financial family connections crossed political lines. The eldest son of Robert Bewick (an avowedly Puritan mayor in 1639) was married to a Maddison. Maddison himself had been mayor in 1632. John Marley, who of course served as Mayor, complained that Maddison 'was one of the greatest favourers of those of faction in all Newcastle but he carries it warily'. George Lilburne with George Grey of Southwark ran Harraton mine on the Wear, with Grey acting as the financial backer. In 1661 both of these were members of another consortium which, with Ralph Lambton and William Belasis, ran the Lambton mines – a mix of gentry and merchants[24]. These local merchant barons formed a web of alliances and established networks which, by their operation, influenced the political allegiance of their membership, post magnatial affinities based on trade and patronage.

Boothmen (corn merchants) brought corn into the town, often in exchange for coal shipped to Kings Lynn. The region between the Tyne and the Tees was not, on the whole, a corn producing area: 'They were not able to serve this town with corne, not three months out of the yeare'[25]. Indeed, Newcastle had an expanding role to play in shipping grain out into the Northumbrian hinterland. In return, the rural areas supplied meat, dairy products, draught animals and raw materials such as leather and tallow. The late sixteenth and early seventeenth centuries was a period of rising population and economic inflation. Landowners thus had an incentive to enclose commons, renegotiate tenancies and develop commercial use of land to boost revenue. Rents thus rose accordingly and many old-style agricultural tenants were eased off the land in favour of new lease holders.

Most Unready – The City Walls

Newcastle, like most major cities, still possessed functioning medieval walls. The tradition of girding urban settlements with a defensive enceinte was an ancient one harking back to Rome and the Celtic oppida the legions overcame. The harsh lessons of the Boudiccan rebellion where sprawling, largely undefended settlements became tombs of their hapless inhabitants exerted a powerful warning against complacency. Newcastle was walled to defend the town primarily against the Scots. The long and bitter centuries of the Three Hundred Years War from 1296 to about 1568 witnessed endemic conflict which flared incessantly at skirmish level and, quite frequently, burst into full-scale conflagration with a litany of major battles; Halidon Hill (1333), Neville's Cross (1346), Otterburn (1388), Homildon (1402), Flodden (1513), Solway Moss (1542) and Pinkie (1547). By the time of the civil wars most of these fortifications, whilst still standing, had been neglected. Only Berwick, with its powerful thrusting bastions, represented the Renaissance ideal of an artillery fort. Medieval walls were not built to withstand shot, indeed they could not. Mighty Norham, which had resisted the Scots for two years in the early fourteenth century, fell after a five-day bombardment from James IV mighty train in 1513.

John Mabbitt points out that the extent and quality of civil war defences, surrounding and augmenting earlier walls is patchy and the archaeological work which has been undertaken to reveal more has not been comprehensive. Most civil war works were thrown up in a hurry and on a budget. Some nonetheless were extremely extensive and complex in form:

By the middle of the seventeenth century many of these medieval walls were in varying states of ruination. Despite some notable refortifications during the sixteenth century, the walls of many towns had begun to decay or had been encroached on by new development. In military terms the medieval walls were obsolete by comparison to the bastioned defences of the Low Countries and Italy which had been built in the sixteenth century[26].

Langton, in looking at patterns of urban settlement, comments that the walls of Newcastle still constituted a form of social demarcation with the poorer sort residing in the suburbs without the enceinte. Writing in the sixteenth century, Leland had noted that, 'The strength and magnificence of the walling of this town [Newcastle] far passes all the walls of the cities of England and of most of the towns of Europe'[27]. As John Mabbitt observes, it had been customary for townsfolk to fund the maintenance of their defences and the mural towers studding Newcastle's ramparts bore the names of individual guilds (see below), this is at least in part confirmed by Gray in his *Chorographia*[28]. Labour, willing or conscripted, was supplied by local residents and artisans and used to raise such outworks as the sconce known as the Shieldfield Fort:

> Thomas Wouldhave appointed overseer of the works. Any who refused to come to pay 8d per day. Everyone to come at six in the morning. A drum to call them and go with them to work. To bring shovels etc to work with. Moved that the town undertake the work of the Shieldfield fort as a testimony of their love and respect for Parliament for funds vouchsafed to the corporation. Ordered that all the earth and sod work to be done by the burgesses at their cost ... To be drawn up and entered at the next Common Council[29].

With the emergence of a new mercantile haute-bourgeois elite in the sixteenth century the walls, intended purely for defence became a symbol of civic identity and pride: 'The key to the continuing importance of the medieval walls was their importance in maintaining civic identity through the embodiment of a legitimacy granted to the town as a corporate body'[30]. This was not mere puff, the walls were, in every sense, a concrete statement of the city's ancient rights, tangible resistance to notions of centralism, be these uttered by King or Parliament. In this we may feel that Newcastle was unique to the degree that other cities had not needed their walls since the Wars of the Roses and even then sieges were very rare. Newcastle, the northern bastion, had maintained its position as a bulwark against the Scots through the sixteenth century. If a major threat from north of the border had largely evaporated after the Treaty of Berwick there was still plenty of low intensity conflict – the Raid of the Reidswire (1575), the destruction of Haydon Bridge (1587) and Scott of Buccleuch's celebrated raid on Carlisle in (1596) being but more notorious examples.

That walls still had a military role was underlined by the debacle of 1640, Conway's ill-judged decision to stand at Newburn left the city completely exposed. Had he perhaps chosen to remain behind the walls, Leven would have faced a far more difficult choice, the dragging drain of a siege or risk of escalade. Damage caused to the walls during the siege and subsequent rebuilding will be discussed elsewhere. Even after the Restoration, when various properties and other 'obstructions' abutting the walls were removed[31], their long service continued and were still able to be put in a defensible state during the last Jacobite alarum in 1745!

In 1644 the walls still stood some 12ft in height, with a thickness of 8ft, and fronted by a ditch or fosse some 22 yards wide and 8ft in depth. Gates were 'embattled' and the enceinte studded with strong towers 'between each of which, there were for the most part two watch towers made square with effigies of men cut in stone upon the top of them as though they were watching, and they are called garret, which had square holes over the walls to through [throw] stones down'[32]. In terms of the overall circumference, Hutton's plan gives a distance of 2,740 yards from Closegate to Sandgate; a later measurement carried out in 1745 which includes the Quayside totals 3,759 yards and one foot[33]! Once the circuit was complete, responsibility for ongoing maintenance was assigned to the twenty-four wards, each responsible for its adjacent gates and intervening towers.

The ward areas were defined as follows, although at least one account states there were twenty-three rather than four[34]:

1. Close Gate	13. Andrew Tower
2. White Friar Tower	14. New Gate
3. Denton or Nevil Tower	15. Bertram Monboucher Tower
4. West Spital Tower	16. Ficket Tower
5. Stank Tower	17. Pilgrim Street gate
6. Gunner Tower	18. Carlell [Carliol] Tower
7. Pink Tower	19. Plummer Tower
8. West Gate	20. Austin Tower
9. Durham Tower	21. Corner Tower
10. Herber Tower	22. Pandon Gate
11. Morden Tower	23. Wallknoll Tower
12. Ever Tower	24. Habkyn Tower

All of the towers were constructed with a rounded outer face and rectangular inner elevation. This was a form designed to frustrate or limit the effectiveness of mining, very much a medieval tactic which was to feature extensively in the siege. In the south-west corner, the circuit commenced with the Riverside Tower, which stood to the left (looking from the inside out) of the Close Gate, from here, on the level riverside, the line ran sharply uphill, broken by the Whitefriar Tower, which derived its name from the adjoining Carmelite Friary (a postern had been knocked through for the convenience of the friars). Here the Masons Guild met in the upper storey whilst the bricklayers used the lower level. Northwards, next to Neville Tower, stood the family's town residence of Westmorland House. Next, the circuit looped off north-west to reach the formidable West Gate which Leland described as 'a mightye strong thing'. It was frequently employed as a gaol – during the civil wars some seventeen prisoners escaped *en masse*, using smuggled ropes to descend via the privies[35]!

None of the quartet of towers along this section have survived. That which ran parallel to Stowell Street, past St Andrew's to the New Gate[36] has fared rather better though, frustratingly, the portal itself has gone. Bourne described it as 'not only the strongest but also the most antient [ancient] of all the other gates'[37]. Herber Tower was the meeting house of the felt makers, curriers and armourers, whilst Morden Tower accommodated glaziers, pewterers, and painters[38] From New Gate the line continued in an easterly direction along the line of Blackett Street to Pilgrim Gate then to Carliol Tower[39]. Here the wall bends south down to the well preserved, though altered, Plummer Tower (Cutler's Guild), past Austin Tower, a corner turret, then Pandon Gate; Wall Knoll Tower (Carpenters), the Sally Port (so called as this was a postern enabling the garrison to mount a raid or sally) and, across City Road to Sand Gate. This was so called as it was built upon the alluvial sands; it was demolished in the eighteenth century as a safety hazard.

In 1644 these noble walls would resume their former significance and become the very symbol of the townspeople's resistance, a fusion of status and function dictated by expediency and dire need! Those of the better sort, the merchant-princes still had their town houses in the old mercantile heart, the Close and Sandhill where stood tall and stately timber-framed houses, lit by casement windows. Waterways such as the Lort Burn which Speed's map of 1610 shows as running north to south through the centre, steep-sided and choked with noxious refuse, were as yet left uncovered[40]. In the Side were many shops and artisans dwellings. Sandhill remained the municipal heart of the city, where coal barons and shippers conducted business and held court. Less prosaically Sandhill also housed the fish-market.

To the north, the Bigg Market, Oat and Flesh Markets teemed, these last two divided by a double row of residential properties with the aptly named Middle Street running centrally between. The Flesh Market was, in part, given over to the sale of cloth – the Cloth Market, which hosted two annual fairs granted by medieval charter[41]. Standing northwards beyond Bigg Market was a residential street, Hucksters' Booths in Newgate Street. East of this lay Pilgrim Street regarded then as being the most agreeable thoroughfare in the city; those of the lesser sort lived beyond the centre in diminishing splendour. So the heart of the medieval plan remained as the jewel with some grand residences such as Anderson Place, built in the wake of the Dissolution on the site of the former Grey Friars, beyond. The streets would have resonated with noise and been narrow, cramped, verminous and reeking. The sixteenth and seventeenth centuries were a period when those of wealth still lived in the centre, though many now did have country houses, the process of sub-urbanisation had not truly begun and the diaspora from the heart lay in the future.

2

Laud's Liturgy

For Church and King he quits his favourite arts,
Forsakes his Knaves, forsakes his Queen of Hearts:
For Church and King he burns to stain with gore
His doublet, stained with nought but sack before.

Anon.

In a retreat besides the honour of the army, the loss is often equal to two battles. For this reason we should never despair while brave men are to be found with their colours. It is by this means we obtain victory, and deserve to obtain it.

Napoleon Bonaparte

The Road towards Civil War

'The most worthy of the title of an honest man'[1] ... an excellent understanding but was not confident enough of it; which made him often times change his own opinion for a worse, and follow the advice of a man that did not judge so well as himself'[2]. Clarendon's judgement of the King is certainly a fair one and Charles' vacillation would cause more spilling of blood that an outright tyrant's ruthlessness. He got off to an unfortunate start, being under the sway of his late father's handsome if empty-headed favourite Buckingham, whose ill-starred foreign policy in the late 1620s exacerbated acute cash shortages and developing differences with Parliament. At a time of marked religious intolerance, Charles stood for a broader acceptance, suspicious in itself. His marriage to a French Catholic Henrietta Maria, a daughter of Henry IV, fuelled fears of a return to abhorrent popery. His faith was based on the tenets of the Arminian Sect[3], and a revival of the Thirty-Nine Articles[4] further stoked Protestant fears of Papist intentions. In March 1629, parliamentary sensitivity reached boiling point with the riotous passage of three resolutions which condemned MPs to eleven years in the wilderness[5].

With Parliament in exile, the groundswell of opposition to the King's perceived abuses of the Royal Prerogative came from town and shire. Gentry disliked poor administration and tradesmen groaned under the escalating burden of unfair taxation; the innocuously named Ship Money[6] was singularly detested by gentleman and commoner, squire, yeoman, merchant and artisan. Presbyterians wished to see a Church of England re-modelled on anti-Episcopalian lines similar to the Scottish Kirk. Puritans[7], whilst remaining within the framework of the Church of England, were not marked for their tolerance. Charles' ruthless arrest and imprisonment of nine MPs[8] and insistence that, as a free prince, he was accountable to God alone and that he was the fountainhead of English liberties, not grasping oligarchs in Parliament, blinded him to the changing realities within society. Despite the haphazard and burdensome nature of these unconstitutional taxes, despite mutterings from town and county and despite the strictures of Charles' nominee Archbishop Laud[9], who antagonised low church sentiment by enforcing measures which, to Puritan and Presbyterian alike smacked of Rome, the administration staggered though the early 1630s.

However, in 1638 two events occurred which were to propel the English polity towards civil strife. John Hampden's refusal to pay the hated Ship Tax and his lukewarm prosecution, with only a bare majority of those on the bench prepared to grit their teeth and bow to the King's right, opened the floodgates and the detested and illegal imposition became progressively unenforceable. Charles might yet have ridden this particular storm had not another, far more tempestuous, arisen north of the border with Scotland.

The King had shown scant interest in his northern realm. He had journeyed there in 1633, some eight years after his coronation in England to be crowned in Scotland. That aside, he showed no more affection for the land of his ancestors than had his father. To be fair, Scotland had been somewhat unkind to the Stuarts[10]. The ham-fisted and ill-conceived attempt to foist a new *Book of Common Prayer* ('Laud's Liturgy'[11]) upon the Kirk produced a tumultuous backlash, with Scots hastening to sign a National Covenant[12]. It is difficult to fathom the King's motives in introducing so controversial a measure at this time. It would seem that these must, as Gardiner observes, have arisen from a naïve passion for order and conformity which paid no heed to, or was ignorant of or indifferent to, potent reality.

Next, Charles sought to browbeat a General Assembly of the Kirk, which rather shouted its defiant outrage and threw fuel onto the fire by taking an even more radical anti-Episcopalian stance. In fact, what the King had accomplished was to promote a strong nationalist opposition within Scotland, united behind the banner of the Kirk and able to field a well-drilled and equipped army led and officered by a cadre of professional soldiers who had learnt their business well in European conflicts[13]. Charles, by contrast, could not afford an army, his efforts to recruit were risible and his weakness obliged him to call for a ceasefire virtually before a shot was fired. The Pacification of Berwick[14] was nothing more than a breathing space. Charles was obstinately determined to enforce his will upon Scotland, resistance which his and Laud's rank folly had sparked. Casting about for sage counsel, the King selected Viscount Strafford[15] as his political and military advisor. To his credit, Strafford saw continued war with Scotland as pernicious but, bowing to the sovereign's will, advised that only by recalling Parliament could Charles garner sufficient resources to recruit an army capable to taking the field.

John Pym was the leading opposition spokesman and the 'Short Parliament' proved to be anything but accommodating. Pym and his growing faction of MPs demanded that Ship Money be debated and dispensed with and that Members privileges must also be on the agenda. Persuaded to compromise, Charles offered to abandon Ship Tax (no grand gesture as the tax was largely un-collectable by now), but MPs were not minded to play along. Having learnt nothing from previous blunders, the King now reasoned he must re-open hostilities without parliamentary support and thus consigned this new, short-lived house to early oblivion. This resumption of hostilities would prove disastrous.

The Rout of Newburn Ford, 28 August 1640

The decision to bully the Scots into submission whilst their available forces were infinitely superior both in numbers and quality was rash to the point of utter recklessness, a strategy of wishful thinking. Lord Conway was appointed to lead a ragtag army consisting of some 12,000 foot and perhaps 3,000 horse. On 21 August, in the late afternoon light, well prepared Scots' regiments, led by Leven, crossed the Tweed. Their numbers are said to have been as high as 27,000, though this seems very high indeed; Mackenzie estimates only 20,000 foot and 2,500 horse[16]. It was the custom, imported from Continental wars, for officers to throw dice to determine who should garner the honour of leading the van. James Graham, Marquis of Montrose was the lucky commander and he had done the Covenant good service in the struggle to date. It is perhaps one of the more marked ironies of the Civil Wars that Montrose, who was to be the scourge of his former confederates during his 'Year of Miracles', should lead the first contingent across the Tweed that summer. So large was the column that by the time the rearguard splashed through the churned waters, it was gone midnight on the 22nd.

During the course of the following week, the army moved by easy stages southwards through Northumberland, taking Wooler, Eglingham and Netherwitton as they marched, the sober grey of their uniform enlivened by a flash of plaid and the blue bonnet with a knot of ribbon above the left ear worn by all[17]. This was no grand chevauchée, such as their grandfathers the reivers might have joyfully undertaken, but a disciplined army on the march, three strong columns in line abreast. Unlike those wild winter storms that would dog the Covenanters in January 1644, the weather was hot and dry. By evening on 26th, the army was crowding around Eachwick. The thirst of so large a host had emptied all local wells and their commissariat stripped every barn and byre for miles around[18]. If a First World War foot battalion of say a thousand men would have been strung out over at least a mile of road on the march then Leven's forces, even if we scale down the numbers drastically, would have required, at the very least, a dozen miles and more.

This was akin to the population of a large city on the move, and for the terrified rustics would have been a truly dreadful sight. For many older Northumbrians this would kindle memories of the days of the Steel Bonnets, even if there would be none alive who could remember a Scottish national army marching unchecked.

In accordance with the niceties of war, Leven politely sent a commanded party, under flag of truce, to request free passage through the town. At this time, gruff Jacob Astley[19] was military governor and he wasted no time in sending the Scots on their way. Leven had neither the means nor the desire to become bogged down in a siege or lose hundreds in an escalade. The Scots were aware that the garrison was substantial in numbers, if less certain in quality. By far the most appealing course of action was to bypass the walls and outflank the defenders. Consequently, on 27 August, the Scots advanced to the high ground along Heddon Law[20]. Summer's thickening light was lit by the thousands of camp fires, locals were allowed to come and go without hindrance or molestation, the more Scottish numbers swelled in the telling the better. Astley was aware the fords at Stella were vulnerable and had placed a single battalion on the northern bank whilst an engineer by the name of Lloyd constructed temporary forts or sconces covering the crossings. Whilst the exact location of these redoubts remains unclear, a surviving map from 1779 names the ground below Hedgefield Church as 'the Forts'. One smaller earthwork was placed to cover the more easterly crossing, whilst those further west were guarded by a more substantial arrangement.

With the Scots drawing near, Conway, on the 26th, had written to the King, then at York with the bulk of his forces, requesting orders; was he to try and hold the line of the Tyne or retreat southwards? If he hoped for the latter, a reply from Strafford, which was carried to him by the celebrated author John Rushworth, was completely unequivocal – the River Tyne must, at all costs, be held. Rushworth caught up with the general and his staff, now at Stella Hall, on the morning of Wednesday 28th. Whilst Conway digested his orders – which can scarcely have been welcome, if not unexpected, Goring hurried in with further news. The Scots were advancing and the fight must now begin in earnest. This proved premature, for neither side actually appeared anxious to begin a shooting match. In fact, both simply watched each other from their respective positions as the sun rose and the heat of another long summer's day settled over the valley.

The village of Newburn's tactical significance was that here lay the first fordable reaches of the river above Newcastle itself. The Tyne was wide and slow moving but much silted up[21] so it would prove no significant obstacle. With steep banks, the lazy waters wound though a nondescript belt of meadow and gorse scrub. Most westerly of the fords was that at Newburn itself where the bridge now spans. This was linked to the next, Riding Ford then, moving further west, Kelso and then Crummel Fords. The third of these lay on the line of the ancient drove road north and is said to have been finished with a bed of stones as far back as Roman times. Crummel (latterly incorrectly linked to Oliver Cromwell), in fact, derives from the Old English expression meaning winding stream or waterway.

Responding to this developing threat and with the advance party having already fallen back across the river, Conway had earlier led out a force of chosen shot, some 3,000 strong, and half as many cavalry. He set up his field headquarters at Stella Hall, having left a commanded party in reserve around Whickham church (probably also intended to act as battle police should any faint-hearts decide to quit). Discipline in the King's army was at best uncertain. Conway had already executed a handful of deserters on Newcastle's Town Moor as a lesson in motivation. The forts, both rudimentary though as near complete as could be managed, were stuffed with a party of shot, 400 strong and four field guns[22]. Dominated by the high ground above and across the water, the myriad flaring fireflies of the enemy's camp, the proud array of assembled banners the English, in their miserable, half-finished works, had little cause for optimism.

Had they seen the Scots at work during the hours of darkness they would have felt uneasier still. Baggage was moved to the rear at Heddon. Marksmen lined the hedges and fields above the fords while cottages and barns provided fire positions. Above the settlement, in the tangle of woods, Leven posted some of his plentiful cannon. One battery was dug in before the church and a second posted on Sentinel Hill to the east. A scattering of the light and handy leather guns[23] were carted virtually to the water's edge, even the church tower was converted into a makeshift gun platform. Some but not all of this industry would have been obvious to Conway and his staff in the morning. Punctilious as ever, Leven sent a messenger splashing forward to entreat the English to let him pass, his sole purpose being the peaceable one of presenting a petition to King Charles. The mighty array of forces lining the north bank clearly gave the lie to any piously expressed notions of pacific intent. This was all for form, so that Leven could later claim he was left with no choice but to fight.

Conway intimated that, though he would permit a delegation to proceed southwards, he would not allow the Scots army to follow. This unnatural calm was shattered by a single, well placed shot. A lone Scottish officer, dressed with some élan for the dour covenanters and sporting a black feathered hat, nonchalantly walked his horse down the banks from Newburn and proceeded to let the thirsty mount drink. Whether this was an innocent gesture from a man who thought that a truce was in force or a far less naïve attempt to casually spy out the English deployment must remain uncertain. At least one Royalist musketeer, and a keen-eyed one at that, decided this fellow's impudence should not continue unchecked and dispatched the Scot with a single round.

Leven responded immediately, sending three squadrons of horse to splash through the receding waters (the Tyne was still tidal up to this point). The Covenanter cavalry were met by a ripple of well-directed fire which drove them back. Now the Scottish guns, largely unobserved thus far, thundered massively in reply. A brisk, if unequal, artillery duel ensued as both sides laid down counter-battery fire in the course of which the makeshift English redoubts, particularly the larger of the two took a fearful battering[24]. Some accounts assert that his guns belched and roared for a good three hours, so the afternoon was well advanced before either side could claim any advantage.

All was not well on the English side, with raw recruits dazed by the fury of the bombardment. For young men dragged from bench or plough, from market stall or counting house this was a most unpleasant experience, one that would have severely tested far more seasoned warriors. Colonel Lunsford, commanding the major fort, could feel the morale of his unwilling heroes ebbing. Plunging fire rained down on his half-finished breastworks. One unlucky shell exploded within the ring and carried off a score of men, maiming more, leaving a hideous tangle of eviscerated, shrieking bundles, shorn of limbs.

There was to be no respite and the badly shaken troops could not be kept to their posts. Ripples of panic swelled into a stream and then a flood, men cast aside weapons and equipment and fled, pell-mell, in mindless terror, despite all urgings and threats from their surviving officers. Guns and fort were abandoned. Leslie swiftly followed up his advantage, dispatching a second body of cavalry over the shrinking waters. As their comrades in the infantry suffered, the English horse had been safely out of range on Stella Haugh. These were true cavaliers, reckless, hard drinking, contemptuous of their foes; refusing to be intimidated by a rabble of Scots. Lord Wilmot now led them forward in a bold bid to restore the crumbling line and secure the abandoned guns. They crashed into Leven's outriders and bundled them across the river, back as far as their own gun line. Even as this gallant charge thundered home Leven had switched his fire to the smaller of the English works, dragging more guns to bolster the battery on Sentinel Hill. The combined weight of shot was unendurable and the rattled defenders soon joined their fellows in full flight[25].

Though both flanks had gone, Wilmot's horse held their ground. With an impressive mix of skill and élan, he crowded a dozen squadrons, their own flanks covered by dense hedges, onto the narrow plain and hurled them at the Scottish Lifeguards. It was now around four and the day was neither won nor lost. A furious melee erupted as milling cavalry hacked and lunged, waters churned to a blood-fringed froth, pistols cracked, and men were hurled from their saddles. Sir Henry Vane, despite a gallant fight, was taken with several of his troop, leaving his ensign, Cornet Porter, amongst the dead. Wilmot fought like a lion. Both sides sustained losses and neither could make headway. Despite the gallantry of the English cavaliers, the loss of both redoubts and the massed flight of infantry had effectively decided the issue. For the most part, the fleeing foot did not pause, pelting back up Stella Banks and scattering through those settlements lining the Old Hexham Road. Scottish foot poured volleys into the flanks of Wilmot's horsemen, who began to disengage and withdraw westwards, still in good order.

Here their commander managed to rally both horse and some elements of the foot, preparing to make a further stand. Such gallantry, whilst commendable, was ultimately doomed. In the fight which followed, the cavaliers were again worsted. Wilmot, his faithful mount 'Sylverside', shot from beneath him, was at last taken, along with Sir John Digby and a number of the other surviving officers. The fugitives were, however, spared the worst of a merciless pursuit which normally characterised such precipitate routs. Leven had won his battle but had no desire to accompany this with wanton slaughter. There was no pursuit and the many prisoners were afforded all the courtesies of war. What was left of the English foot, collecting the party left earlier at Whickham, with only a couple of guns salvaged, trudged into Newcastle by nightfall, while the cavalry remnant galloped off to Durham. Conway took the decision to follow with the foot, marching at 5 o'clock next morning[26].

The Scots took possession of the field, giving thanks to God for their victory. Despite the fury of the fight, casualties overall had been light. Perhaps three score English died in the redoubts, with the horseman probably bringing the butcher's bill to not much more than 100. The Scots claimed, undoubtedly rightly, that they had lost less, most of their own casualties being sustained in the cavalry melee. Newcastle was, however, totally unguarded – and to the victor the spoils. It was, as Clarendon described, 'an infamous and irreparable rout'[27].

The Occupation

When Newcastle upon Tyne was taken by the covenanters in the year 1640, the coal trade, which before that event is said to have employed ten thousand people, sustained an immense loss; everyone fled, thinking the Scots would give no quarter, and more than a hundred vessels that arrived off Tynemouth-Bar the day after the fight [Newburn Ford] hearing that the Scots were in possession of the town, returned empty[28].

Conway's defeat and subsequent retreat left the city totally exposed. Jacob Astley remained but reckoned that, without adequate forces, he could not hope to resist the triumphant Scots so 'sunk his ordnance in the river'[29]. Next morning, the Douglas Sheriff of Teviotdale with a body of horse rode in unopposed and formally summoned the town to surrender. He was greeted by the dour acquiescence of total silence, the coal trade, life blood of the city was suspended and many of the more vociferous Royalists had fled. Sir Nicholas

Cole, then mayor, putting a best face upon necessity, ground his teeth to offer the Scottish officers civility and entertain them at table. No northerner was ever likely to welcome the Scots, memories of their reiver grandfathers' still too fresh and ancient grudge sharpened afresh by the sour bile of defeat.

On Sunday 30 August one of the authors of the covenanti, Alexander Henderson, preached a Presbyterian service in St Nicholas' Church whilst the officers sought quarter and the army was encamped in orderly manner on Gateshead Hill[30]. On 1 September Leslie demanded rations of bread and ale from the burgesses for his hungry troops. The mayor dug his heels in so the Scot shrugged his shoulders and took what he needed, though part payment in coin was offered with the balance met by the issue of promissory notes. The covenanters behaved impeccably, maintaining that their sole purpose was to demand redress of their grievances and assurance of their liberties.

As the occupiers settled in, the matter of provisions became inevitably more acute and the following Thursday Leven summoned the Sheriff of Durham and Sir William Lambton to discuss the county's contribution. As the Scots prepared to march southwards a garrison of 2,000 under the Earl of Lothian was left in Newcastle whilst the region prepared to meet a hefty bill of £850 per day to feed and maintain the Scots[31]. This was punitive but the alternative was far more terrifying. Sieges could and did end in a bloodbath, the payment of such a fine, however swingeing, was a sound investment against plunder and free quarter.

For a full year Newcastle suffered the indignity of occupation whilst King and Parliament dithered till finally the Covenanters were bought off with a whopping £300,000 bribe, more carefully expressed as a contribution towards the costs of their valued 'brotherly assistance'[32]. On 10 August, King Charles passed through the city on his way north to negotiate with his unruly Scottish subjects, returning the same way on 19 November. In fairness the burgesses had little to complain of other than the costs. In fact, the orderly conduct of the Scots contrasts with that of Conway's disreputable host, many of whom openly sympathised with the Presbyterians, some going so far as to murder their officers. The register of St Andrew's Church records that 'two soldiers, for denying the King's pay, was, by a council of war, appointed to be shot at, and a pair of gallows set up before Thos Malaber's door in the Bigg-Market. They cast lots which should die, and the lots did fall of one Anthone Viccars; and he was set against a wall, and shot at by 6 light horsemen, and was buried in our churchyard the same day, May 16 day'[33]. When the Scots finally marched north the citizens would doubtless have heaved a corporate sight of relief, believing their difficulties were now at an end.

They would have been quite wrong.

3

The Gathering Storm

Thank Heaven! At last the trumpets peal
Before our strength gives way.
For King or for the Commonweal-
No matter which they say.
The first dry rattle of new-drawn steel,
Changes the world today.

'Edgehill Fight' Rudyard Kipling

It is an approved maxim of war, never to do what the enemy wishes you to do, for this reason alone, that he desires it.

Napoleon Bonaparte

Raising the King's Standard

One important consequence of the Treaty of Ripon, signed in October 1640, was to oblige Charles to recall Parliament next month, the 'Long Parliament'. The dire fiasco of the Second Bishops' War had only served to exacerbate the swelling tide of opposition which now embraced the majority of MPs. Many who would continue to serve the King and even die beneath his banners were, at this stage antagonised[1]. Strafford became the prime culprit and one to feel the wrath of an outraged polity, Pym moved for his impeachment and the King, though he did not wish to see so loyal a servant lose his head, was also in need of scapegoats. Nobly, the earl volunteered his own neck as means to defuse the rising clamour. Charles had not the ruthlessness to throw his man outright to the wolves, nor the resolution to stand by him. Besides, Pym wanted more – he demanded that Parliament must, by statute, meet every five years. On 20 May 1641 Strafford paid the price of loyalty to the Stuart cause. He would not be the only one to find the gratitude of kings somewhat unpredictable and totally unreliable.

Neither Pym himself nor even the more vociferous members could, at this point, be described as revolutionaries. They sought to limit the powers of the monarch, to force recognition of Parliament's role as principal advisor, but none was seeking to remove the King as figurehead, at least not yet. With Strafford gone and the King humiliated, the summer of 1641 witnessed a series of concessions, including the abolition of Ship

Money and the passing of the Triennial Act[2]. Some now, however, began to drift towards a view that sufficient reforms had been undertaken. This fragile balance was derailed by the outbreak of rebellion in Ireland[3].

This fresh crisis seemed set to tilt the balance of power further in Parliament's favour. Pym began to suggest that royal appointees be subject to assent from the legislature and that defence should properly be a matter for Parliament rather than remain within the bounds of the royal prerogative. Pym and the reformers pressed their suit with the 'Grand Remonstrance', essentially a complaint of Parliament against all of the Crown's perceived injustices since Charles came to the throne; this at a time when the King sought to uphold *The Book of Common Prayer* and extend patronage by the appointment of further bishops.

Charles, with a classic gift for mistiming, decided now was the time for action and a heavy hand. On 4 January 1642 he entered Parliament and sought the arrest of five members[4]. All were forewarned and had judiciously slipped away beforehand. The monarch, thus confounded, cast about for what to do next. Charles had no true strategy for dealing with the opposition but felt sufficiently isolated and threatened to abandon Whitehall for the less perilous bounds of Hampton Court. This began the inexorable countdown to armed confrontation, more of a slide than an avalanche but a process, once put in train, which neither faction appeared able to halt. Reason was being ousted by belligerence. The parties were squaring up to each other for want of any safer notions and with no apparent understanding of the consequences of their actions. The Dogs of War, once loosed, are mighty hard to recall.

As battle lines were being drawn, with the queen sent on a mission to the Continent to procure arms, fitful negotiations persisted. By March, however, Pym was pressing for the contentious Militia Ordinance[5]. This would have wrested control of the armed forces, or what passed for armed forces, from the King, a step too far. By the spring Charles had abandoned Hampton Court and established himself with what was, in effect, the nucleus of a war council in York. Parliament's demands became more rather than less radical; the 'Nineteen Propositions' sought to strip the Crown of virtually all constitutional power. Charles' advisors sought to bargain but, by July, the navy, now commanded by the Earl of Warwick and leaning heavily toward the Parliamentary cause, was joined by an army to be raised by the earl of Essex[6]. The King had blunderingly attempted to gain control of the important arsenal at Hull, where the governor, Sir John Hotham[7], defied him. This was a largely bloodless affair but a confrontation by any standards and on, 22 August, the anniversary of Bosworth Field (perhaps an inauspicious precedent), the King formally raised his banners at Nottingham. The English Civil War had begun.

Course of the War: 1642 – Opening Moves

From the outset, the Parliamentarian army under Essex broadcast that it fought not against the person of the anointed King but against those malign counsellors about him, a small but important distinction. Charles, if frustrated and significantly weakened by his inability to secure arms, received a potent boost to his cause when joined by his nephews Rupert and Maurice[8], who brought not just their swords but vital armaments. Neither faction was prepared for a war, which had taken the nation by surprise.

England's halcyon days when the men of the grey goose feather dominated battlefields across Europe were long gone and there had been no serious domestic fighting south of the borders since Stoke Field.

On the Continent, the art of war had undergone a major transformation in the sixteenth century. It was now the age of pike and shot. Initially, Swiss pike blocks and then the Spanish Tercio had been the dominant deployments till Dutch and Swedish innovations successfully challenged the latter. The day of the Tercio was not yet over in 1642 but Conde's great victory at Rocroi the following year was to prove decisive. Aside from those, and there were many, particularly in Scotland, who had seen active service in the Thirty Years War[9], few Britons had much experience of these new ways of waging war. The Elizabethan Revolution had been a naval rather than land-based phenomenon.

Rupert showed his mettle during the first clash at Powicke Bridge on 23 September where he successfully beat a Parliamentarian force. Good news was needed for Portsmouth had been lost and Essex's army was growing and on the march. The King was able to draw support from the Welsh marches and the north. His march south from Shrewsbury, commencing on 12 October, persuaded his enemies to secure the capital, relying on a sizeable force drawn from the well-equipped trained bands. Essex, who had himself marched to Northampton, endeavoured to interdict the Royalist advance. On 23 October, learning their foes were close, the King's army drew up in battle array at Edgehill. This was far from seamless, being disordered by most unseemly squabbles within the Royalist leadership. Prince Rupert was a dashing and competent commander but his youth, impatience and Germanic bluntness did not endear him to his uncle's older, more cautious officers. The King's army by now comprised some 10,000 foot, 3,000 horse and perhaps 1,000 dragoons. Essex could field rather less cavalry and dragoons but rather superior numbers of infantry[10].

The first battle of the English Civil War which both parties felt would be decisive was not. It was a rather groping and blundering affair. Initially, the Royalists, who advanced first to contact, appeared to have the upper hand though victory was denied partly by the recklessness of their horse and partly by a determined stand by the remnant of those Parliamentarian foot regiments which had not already fled. The net result was one of bloodied stalemate. Essex's army, on balance, had fared rather worse but he had relief approaching and the King's advance against London appeared thwarted.

Charles had cause to be resolute and bold but avoided the test by preferring to establish his headquarters at Oxford, while Parliament was afforded leisure to recover. Then, the Royalist march upon London was resumed with Rupert securing Brentford in fine style on 12 November, but Parliament was ready, barring the road with impressive numbers drawn up at Turnham Green. Some Royalists believed the King should have battered his way through and that the trained bands would not stand. In this they might have been correct but Charles chose not to enter his capital in a tide of blood.

As the campaigning season of 1642 spluttered to an unsatisfactory close, neither side had any grounds for self-congratulation. Parliament had narrowly avoided losing the war and the King was growing three field armies; his own at Oxford, the Marquis of Newcastle's in the north and Sir Ralph Hopton's[11] in the far south-west. The Marquis of Newcastle, advised by Lord Eythin and Goring, had occupied York. If the King's generals showed some energy and drive, both he and they were continually hamstrung by an acute cash shortage. Parliament, if on the back foot, had the capacity to levy a property-based tax across all the districts they controlled and which, in the main, tended to comprise the wealthier counties. Charles was constrained to rely upon loans or donations from his followers, such credit as the Queen could secure abroad and the evils of free quarter.

A View from the Tyne

To comprehend how cities like Newcastle upon Tyne were governed, we need to develop an understanding of civic and administrative functions of the time. Guilds were instruments of access to participation in civic life and exemplars of the completely enmeshed relationships between economic and social organisation[12]. Town governance was a complicated construction which had evolved over time. By the mid-seventeenth century the structure broadly encompassed the mayor, sheriff, Common Council, composed of aldermen, of whom the mayor was one, and the Twenty-Four. This latter body was returned by a series of seven elections held on an annual basis. The representatives were generally drawn from the twelve 'mysteries' (the major trading concerns). The numbers involved in each of the seven elections reduced as each ballot was completed; the victors in the last going on to nominate the candidates for the next. To add complexity to an already intricate process, the pool of those eligible for election expanded as each ballot progressed in that, candidates could now be drawn from outside the twelve mysteries.

The Guild, an assembly of all the burgesses of the town, constituted on three fixed occasions during the year, was a powerful influence. Alongside and deeply embedded in these structures was an inner ring, formally recognised by a charter of Queen Elizabeth I from 1597 sanctioning their control of the town's government and economic control of the Northern region[13]. This inner ring or cabal was very largely made up from the Hostmen (coal traders), whose influence derived from their monopolistic control over river traffic and the considerable income to be derived from it. Howell[14] observes that the oligarchs of this inner circle, exercising substantive control and seeking to ensure Newcastle's continuing privileges at the expense of neighbouring localities (both along the river and regionally e.g. Gateshead, Durham, Shields), were generally drawn from the Merchant Adventurers and/or Mercers (influential traders with a maritime connection) as well as hostmen. Merely being a hostman was of itself insufficient. Elizabeth's charter had recognised *de facto* control of the town by this elitist inner ring of the Court of Common Council – effectively the trade bodies and guilds of the town. The complex electoral rules did not award a place to the hostmen as a separate body.

This charmed inner circle of say, a score of hostmen, exerted political and economic control as members of local society in the Tyne Valley, having previously intermarried with gentry (the Blacketts being a prime example). Newcastle was their commercial heart even if it was no longer, in numerous instances, their principal dwelling. At the centre of the town's economic dominance they naturally had a vested interest in maintaining its mercantile privileges. Their power and influence was embedded rather than imposed[15]. These various components of town government could and did use the sheer complexity of election arrangements to frustrate business. Ensuring a meeting was not quorate was seen as a deliberate strategy by the Butcher's company: 'by reason whereof the said election was not only obstructed and the electors affronted but the peace and charter of this Corporation exceedingly endangered'[16]. By giving effective control to an inner ring, the charters of Elizabeth I and James I had created a dissenting minority of those townsmen who formed an actual majority and who wished to see control vested in the Guild.

A continued series of attacks on the inner ring fostered by this resentment were a by no means an insignificant factor during the build up to the civil war. For example, a riot by apprentices in March 1633 appeared, on the surface, to constitute a protest about the siting of a lime kiln on ground they used for drying clothes. Mayor and justices wrote a letter of complaint to Lord Chief Justice Coke, Secretary of State, advising they had received little aid from the burgesses who had secretly sided with the rioters. Coke agreed, making a note that the real cause of the disturbance was likely to have been a desire by the commons of the town to effect a change in governance.

In June 1633, a deputation of four burgesses journeyed to London bearing a weighty petition signed by 700 of their fellows. Grievances listed were that: the mayor and aldermen consistently refuse to hear grievances from the remainder of the burgesses presented at a meeting of the Guild; the mayor and aldermen routinely do not come to Guild meetings until after 10 a.m. and leave as soon as anything touching upon grievances arises! Profits from the sale of offices such as the town clerkship, which should have been utilised to benefit the town and preserve the river, were being used for personal purposes by the mayors themselves (the matter of £200 taken by William Warmouth during his time in office was cited). Membership of the Common Council had been so rigged that only four or at most six of the twenty-four represented the common burgesses. The rest comprised friends and relatives of the mayor and aldermen. The burgesses now demanded that privileges of the freemen be preserved to prevent non freemen trading within the town. Further, amendments to the quorum of the Common Council were sought to limit power within this charmed inner circle[17].

The King was unable to consider the petition since he was at the time in Newcastle being entertained by the very people complained of! A second attempt to present the petition to him at Berwick led to him sending it on to the Council of the North, whose august members airily dismissed such overtures as typical complaints from those of mean condition 'who are apt to turn every pretence and colour of grievance into uproar and seditious mutiny'.[18] With such sweeping condescension the Council quietly allowed the matter to lapse. Opposition to the policies of the inner ring did not always go hand in hand with opposition to the Royal Prerogative. All mercantile factions were united in their opposition to Ship Money, with the burgesses rallying round the Common Council after the first two levies. An assault on the purses of some was an assault upon the coffers of all.

Religious differences provided an additional source of friction in the town. The two did not always go hand in hand of course. Robert Bewick, occupying the office of mayor on the eve of civil war, was Puritan, a hostman and a mercer, a longstanding member of the inner ring. Contact with London (and with the emerging radical religious ideas of the capital) was easiest amongst the merchant class who traded with the city. These were well educated and cosmopolitan and it was amongst this influential group which included luminaries such as John Blakiston, John Cousins and Henry Dawson that Puritan notions began to emerge.

As in the current epoch, growth in commerce, particularly the coal trade, brought a class of migrant workers into the city. We have seen the results of population change in our own time and this was a group who were particularly likely to be vociferous and hard to manage: 'This potentially unruly and miscreant immigrant workforce was juxtaposed against the cultural sophistication of those belonging to Newcastle's upper echelons'[19]. This largely unheard migrant class would have a role to play during the siege, for example. They protest when they are dragged away from their normal occupations to build forts and dig defences – attempts to force them to do so result in a near riot. It could be argued these recent economic immigrants have far less embedded affinities within the town and a greater sense of their own independence.

Conformity and Dissent

Distance from London meant local priests were removed from effective central control and perhaps more recusant in their practices that would otherwise have been the case. The wild reaches of North Tynedale were truly distant from the Episcopal seat of Durham and local gentry, names resonating from the dark days of the steel bonnets, exercised more control than any bishop. Allied to a certain innate and xenophobic conservatism were a cadre of poorly educated clergy serving very large parishes (Newcastle had only four) and often subject to rumours of incompetence or poor behaviour.

At the same time as the mercantile elite were becoming versed in new ideas radiating outwards from the capital, easy access to the ports and the frequent comings and goings from the Continent made a convenient staging post for Catholic priests, nuns, books and tracts – particularly those heading for the homes of recusant families such as the Howards, Widdringtons and their affinities. Social and family connections protected many of these families and would lead the Parliamentarians and Scots alike to complain of the malignant (popish) nature of the city and the Earl of Newcastle's army. Nonetheless, there was clearly a strong anti-catholic element within the Corporation. In 1630 Zacharias van der Steen of Liege complained he had been imprisoned in the town jail for three years because the French ship which had given him passage was suspected of transporting priests! This was not an isolated incident.

From the beginning of the seventeenth century there are traces of Puritan lecturers in the town associated with the churches of St Nicholas and All Saints. Activity seems to have been largely individual – transient preachers coming and then going without establishing any significant following until the arrival of Dr Robert Jennison in the 1630s. It is then that a significant Puritan opposition may be seen to arise. His family was both local and well connected – father and uncle had been mayors. Dissent focussed initially on resisting what were viewed as the Arminian policies of Durham. Jennison was opposed to what he regarded as 'popish innovations' – this, amongst other accusations, led him into conflict with the corporation. In alliance with local merchants such as Dawson, Maddison and Blakiston, he helped form a significant dissenting faction, based on social, family and trading networks. For example, the Puritan mayor, Robert Bewick's eldest son, was married to Maddison's sister; Maddison himself had been mayor in 1632. Sir John Marley, complained that Maddison 'was one of the greatest favourers of those of faction in all Newcastle but he carries it warily'[20].

Connections between Newcastle Puritans and Scots Covenanters led to investigation and repression, particularly as disputes over the role of the bishops escalated. The dissenters were able to force through the election of a Puritan mayor in open defiance of the King who was then left with no option but to invite him to London. The inevitable backlash forced the two most notable preachers to flee northwards in 1639/1640. Scots' occupation of the city seemed likely to offer a replacement to the missing leadership but matters moved against the Puritans almost immediately. The Scots, of course, were far from welcome, that ancient and detested foe. Association with them, even by proxy, condemned those citizens who might, on religious grounds, have welcomed them … 'The common soldiers are intolerably insolent and violent in their actions'. Far from reinforcing the position of the radical religious element, occupation started to turn their fellow citizens against them.

A Puritan of sixteenth and seventeenth-century England was most likely an associate of any number of religious groups advocating more 'purity' of worship and doctrine, as well as personal and group displays of piety. Puritans felt that the English Reformation had not gone far enough, and that the Church of England was tolerant of practices which they associated with Catholicism. The Church of England as a whole was perceived as too close to Catholicism for austere and suspicious Puritans. The movement was distinctive from the rest of the Church in theology, even more prescriptive than dour Calvinism, in legalism, theonomy and especially – congregationalism. Charles as King was determined to scourge these 'excesses' of Puritanism from the body of the Church of England. His close advisor, William Laud, Archbishop of Canterbury from 1633, moved the established Church still further away from Puritanism, rigorously enforcing laws against schismatic ministers who dared deviate from the *Book of Common Prayer* or who violated the ban on preaching on predestination.

Puritans opposed much of the Calvinist summations in the Church of England, notably the *Book of Common Prayer*, but also the use of non-secular vestments (cap and gown) during services, the use of the Holy Cross during baptism, and kneeling during the sacrament. Puritans rejected anything they thought smacked of popery. Whilst Puritans in the reign of James I attempted to sway peaceful reform of the Church of England, James viewed their religious beliefs as close to heresy, and their denial of Divine Right as potentially treasonous.

Charles' consort, Henrietta-Maria de Bourbon of France, was so extreme in her devotion to the Pope that she refused to attend her husband's coronation. She certainly had no love for Puritans. Laud also detested Puritans, viewing them as a threat to established orthodoxy. Charles relied largely on the Star Chamber and the Court of High Commission. Although these were venerable institutions, Charles tinkered with their function to suppress Puritanism. These were prerogative courts constituted under the direct control of the sovereign, not of Parliament and were handy for convicting and imprisoning those who, though they had not violated any statute, had incurred royal displeasure. As a result, large numbers of Puritans emigrated *en masse* to New England, an exodus dubbed 'the Great Migration'. The rump of the movement in England allied itself with the cause of 'England's ancient liberties'. Laud's increasing unpopularity and the continued suppression of Puritanism were major factors leading to Civil War.

Newcastle Prepares

As the certainty of hostilities swelled in the early months of 1642, both sides were naturally anxious to secure so vital a commercial centre as Newcastle. Parliament issued an edict to this effect on 19 March (*see* appendix 7). A naval squadron was assembled to, if necessary, blockade the Tyne but the Earl of Newcastle had already received his sovereign's commission to secure the north-east. He acted speedily, sending some 600 foot, drawn from the trained bands, with a hundred horse to secure Durham. A commanded party half that number but bolstered by six guns[21] was dispatched to commence fortification of the southern flank of the river's wide mouth at South Shields. Appraised of these moves, Parliament dispatched two men of war to frustrate Newcastle's efforts and 'to prevent the inconveniences that may happen by the fort therein building'[22].

The earl's deployments appeared to accord with the wishes of the burgesses, who included him as an honorary member and sent a donation of £700 to swell the royal coffers[23]. In September Parliament riposted, judging that Cole, Sir Thomas Riddell the younger, Sir Alexander Davison, Sir John Marley and Thomas Liddell be considered 'delinquents'[24]. At the time, this was easier in the passing than the enforcing and a further prohibition soon followed aimed at preventing the import of arms – in October a Royalist vessel had landed a thousand stands of arms and £10,000 for the King[25].

Royal Visits

In the course of his reign, Charles I visited Newcastle on four occasions, all in very different circumstances. In 1633 he was *en route* to his coronation in the northern kingdom; six year later his relations with Scotland had deteriorated drastically. In 1641 matters were rather worse for the Scots were still in occupation. By 1646–7, the man who had ridden through to be crowned came for the last time as a prisoner. For the first grand visit, every preparation was made, surveyors hurriedly reported on the state of roads and bridges. On Monday 3 June, the King passed from Durham towards Newcastle which the royal party reached that evening. In his glittering train rode several magnates; the Earls of Northumberland, Arundel, Pembroke, Southampton, the Marquis of Hamilton, Dr Laud and many others of note[26]. Few details of the festivities planned for so august a company have survived but the loyal burgesses will have been out to impress. On the next evening the King dined with Mayor Ralph Cole, who received a knighthood[27]. On 5 June the royal guest and his retinue were rowed down the river to Tynemouth in the company of the master and brethren of Trinity House.

Edward Bulmer, who had the honour to be steersman, took the opportunity to press a petition from the brethren to right a previous injustice. This arose from a local dispute (as previously described). Charles' visit to Shields on that day was probably prompted by this dispute which, however, was still smouldering six years later in 1640. The King had already received, the day previously, a further petition from the burgesses alleging the major and aldermen were ignoring their just complaints[28] Rushworth confirms that the citizens provided due entertainment and spectacle befitting so noble and elevated a guest but, frustratingly, offers no detail[29].

Six years later, matters stood very differently. Charles' Scottish subjects were in outraged rebellion. His writ effectively ceased at Berwick upon Tweed, where Leven had stationed substantial covenanting forces, far superior to anything the King could hope to field. On Sunday 5 May, Charles listened to Dr Morton preach a sermon in Durham which sought to remind all worshippers of the King's place in the firmament. Regrettably, the Scots were no longer listening. Sir Jacob Astley, redoubtable military governor of Newcastle appears to have already prepared a billeting plan for the King's forces in and around the city[30]. The mayor had, on 2 April, issued an ordinance intended to cajole citizens into ensuring their town looked its absolute best: 'Whereas his majesty intends shortly, God willing, to be at this town and it is very fitting and necessary that the streets should be clean and sweet, it is therefore ordered that every inhabitant shall make the front of his house and shop clean presently and so from time to time keep the same.' Those who failed to heed were subject to a fine of 8*s* 8*d* (44p); no mean sanction[31].

Astley, ever an experienced and constant soldier, had been making preparations for the city to serve as the King's forward base. He'd ordered brass guns brought from Tynemouth and mounted on new carriages[32], he was refurbishing iron guns already on the walls. He requested 2,500 stands of arms to equip the county-trained bands from both Northumberland and Durham and to arm citizens as required. Intriguingly, he also reports 'we are still inquisitive after the faction of the Puritans to dissolve their meetings'[33] Clearly the dissenters are regarded as a threat. There had obviously been attempts by the covenanters to spread propaganda:

> Last Saturday night, many books were thrown here into houses and in the streets, and under cover of letters sent to citizens of this town. Many of them were also thrown upon the highways in Northumberland ... We assembled the preachers and required them to preach obedience to the people, and find one Dr Jenison something cool, but have not a staff sufficient to question him ...[34].

Astley was most thorough, requiring ship owners to ensure their mariners were armed and ready. He remained aware of the strategic significance of the ford at Newburn which could be bridged by pontoons to facilitate transportation of heavy guns. A leading military engineer, named de Bois, was dispatched by the King during April to supervise the strengthening of the city's defences. Doubtless the burgesses attempted to repeat their displays of hospitality and civic pride exhibited during the earlier visit but again there are few details. We do know that on 8 May 'Sir William Saville past through the town ... with his regiment all clad in red coats, and the men were very much commended, but their arms indifferent'[35]. All was not entirely calm behind the pomp and show. The King's army was woefully inadequate and Sir John Marley hints in correspondence that there are disaffected elements: 'The Ipswich Puritans have so wrought with the ship men, that for six weeks I did not load one chaldron of coals, so that my staiths are so full they are like to fire … I had one fire last year'[36].

Another correspondent, Edward Norgate, wrote of the army's preparations for the march to Berwick: 'To Morpeth is our first remove, thence to Alnwick and Belford, all poor, contemptible villages … And there is no safe stay, where a pestilential fever reigns, and smallpox everywhere'[37]. Bevil Grenville, who was to fight and die in Hopton's army, wrote on 15 May that the city was full of soldiers with more billeted around, yet he observes the army is still short on numbers being 'not yet very strong'. In the midst of all this martial fervour the King was still able to undertake a survey of the city's churches to ascertain that they complied with his requirements for 'decency and order'. In the cases of both St Nicholas' and All Saints', galleries which were likely to block an unimpeded view of the altar were ordered to be struck down[38].

Terry points out as a fascinating anecdote that the Earl of Arundel writing to the Secretary of State on 20 April to dispatch a printer and press to Newcastle 'to set out his majesty's daily commands for his court or army, and that to be done with more than ordinary diligence, the want being daily found so great'[39]. Robert Barker, already contractor to the King, was soon on his urgent way north and the text of Dr Morton's 5 May service became the first tract to roll off his press. On 16 May he produced a more detailed pamphlet, 'Laws and Ordinances of Warre, For the Better Government of this Majesties Army Royall, in the Present Expedition for the Northern parts and safety of the Kingdom'. Despite its long-winded title, this was a carefully constructed code of regulations which in part belies the notion the King's army was altogether ramshackle, though of course these minute provisions were very likely more honoured in the breach than the observance. Rather optimistically, careful guidance was provided on the distribution of spoil or prizes, loot essentially. These proved rather superfluous in a campaign where as one commentator acidly observed, 'I never heard so much as one louse killed by either army'[40].

When next Charles I came to Newcastle circumstances were rather less congenial. The martial pomp of 1639 had turned to mere flatulence after the hasty truce at Berwick and the Scots had trounced the King's threadbare forces at Newburn. Newcastle was now their prize, citizens groaning under the yoke of occupation by an ancient and detested foe – never in the long centuries of border war had the Scots succeeded in taking the city. It was the most abject of humiliations for both King and northern English. Parliament had adroitly used the fact of their allies' presence on English soil as a branch with which to beat the King. By the time Charles came north in August 1641, terms for withdrawal had been negotiated. This must have been bitter gall to Charles, his attempts to foist the prayer book upon the Scots in tatters, his authority in England demeaned, his loyal servants Laud and Strafford in dire jeopardy.

Charles arrived in Newcastle on the 13th of the month, suitably inauspicious we might say. Leven had drawn up his full army in impressive parade formation; 'drew out his whole force, both horse and foot with the Artillery the better to express the soldiers salute and welcome of their King'[41]. The Scottish General, in a wonderful display of showmanship ceremonially dismounted before his sovereign and 'prostrated himself and service before the King upon his knees, his Majestie awhile talking to him and at his rising gave him his hand to kiss, and commanded his horse be given him, whereon remounted, he rode with the King through the army'[42]. The pamphleteer goes on to give a detailed description of the Scottish army. In the first rank Leven had placed his highlanders or 'Redshanks'[43], described as being armed with bows and swords. Next stood bodies of mixed pike and shot, interspersed with galloper guns. The heavy artillery was massed in the centre 'about 60 pieces of Ordnance' with gunners and matrosses standing by their guns. As their royal inspector passed a salute was fired. At once this was both a show of loyalty and a demonstration of might.

Terry places the Scottish camp at this time on the Gateshead side 'at Reidheuche' (Redheugh)[44], which the occupiers had fortified to cover the southern approaches. A week or so later on the 21st, the Scots began the march home. This, like the entire campaign was conducted in a most orderly manner and the occupation does not seem to have engendered any particular grievances. Indeed, having set the army on its way, Leven and his officers briefly returned to insist that, 'if any of the Town were not yet satisfied for anything due to them from officers of soldiers, let them [citizens] bring their Tickets [requisitions] and he would pay them, which he did accordingly'[45].

In 1646 Charles made his final visit (of which more later), except that on this last occasion he was in even worse case, a defeated prisoner, the war ended and his cause in ruins.

War in the North 1642–3

To horse! To horse! Brave Cavaliers
To horse for Church and Crown! Strike, strike your tents! Snatch up your spears!
And ho for London town!

Macaulay

A general of ordinary talent occupying a bad position, and surprised by a superior force, seeks his safety in retreat; but a great captain supplies all deficiencies by his courage, and marches boldly to meet the attack.

Napoleon Bonaparte

The Marquis takes the Field

During this early stage of the Civil Wars, whilst both sides fumbled in the dark of unpreparedness campaigning in the north was, to a very large extent, conducted independently. Charles had appointed the Earl of Newcastle as commander-in-chief and his fiefdom covered all of the northern counties – Cumberland, Westmorland, Northumberland, the Bishopric of Durham and the city of Newcastle upon Tyne. The earl, as he then was, received his commission as early as June but his most urgent mission would be to provide safe haven for the Queen upon her return from the Continent. From the outset then Newcastle upon Tyne's strategic significance lay in its location as a major east coast port where arms and supplies could be brought in without interference.

The city's position was made more critical by virtue of the fact that, with the exception of Chester, it was one of the few significant ports not in Parliamentarian hands[1]. Chester looked west towards Ireland rather than Europe and the quays of Newcastle were swiftly loaded with arms and ordnance. Rupert had disembarked at Tynemouth in August and this traffic continued despite the best attentions of Parliament's ships. The effect on the coal trade was immediate and economically damaging – the cessation also had a practical impact on the capital. The blockade was a formal tactic employed to deny Royalist supply vessels access to the Tyne.

There are some questions as to how effective the blockade was, doubtless in the normal run of things, some skippers could have been persuaded to look the other way at chosen moments[2]! One aspect of trade which was stifled was the movement of coal and that worked in the King's favour in that it deprived London of its primary source of fuel, thus spreading hardship amongst his enemies. Unemployment undoubtedly gave a boost to Newcastle's recruiting. Northumberland and Durham, apart from some rumblings from the trained bands there, remained calm, but in Yorkshire he faced the Fairfaxes.

The War in Yorkshire

Charles had left the Earl of Cumberland, seconded by Sir Thomas Glemham, as local commanders in York but the bulk of locally raised forces had marched south with his nascent field army. In the West Riding Lord Fairfax was recruiting under the aegis of a Militia Ordinance from Parliament. Sir John Hotham was still strongly posted in Hull and Sir Hugh Cholmley had thrown a garrison into Scarborough. It was natural that Cumberland should appeal to Newcastle for aid as he risked being surrounded. The latter was in a rather delicate position, his writ did not extend to Yorkshire and his primary responsibility was to ensure the Queen's safety. And there was the matter of resources; Newcastle was no soldier but he was a canny businessman. His proposal or 'propositions' were that the Yorkshire Royalists should meet the costs of his army whilst he reserved the right to draw off as necessary to succour the Queen. The Fairfaxes had raised their standard in October but it was a month later before Newcastle, his bargaining complete, deigned to march. The forces available to him were probably no more than 4,000 foot and half as many horse[3].

A preliminary skirmish took place on 1 December, when the Royalist van encountered the younger Hotham at Piercebridge and forced the crossing, pushing the smaller Parliamentarian force aside, although the Roundheads seemed to have got clear with modest loss. Fairfax had by now occupied Tadcaster, rather closer to York than was comfortable. Newcastle launched a series of what turned out to be uncoordinated strikes against the town and its garrison which, though they failed to trap the Parliamentarians, ensured they were glad to withdraw largely unscathed. To sidestep Royalist horse, the Fairfaxes moved into Selby, rather than westwards into their heartland.

Newcastle appeared in no particular haste to follow, taking Pontefract Castle and launching an abortive escalade on Bradford. The earl had entrusted operations in the West Riding to Sir William Savile, a nephew of Strafford's and, in Gardiner's opinion, of an equally arrogant disposition[4]. The Royalists did, however, succeed in occupying Newark, a vital bastion and communications gateway. Not to be outdone, 'Black Tom' Fairfax battered his way into Leeds, obliging Newcastle to quit both Pontefract and Wakefield. Sir Thomas Fairfax was to emerge as a pivotal figure, Gardiner, for one, is openly adulatory; 'No more gallant spirit bore arms in the Parliamentary ranks'[5]. By now the campaigning season was well into extra time and Newcastle seemed ready to hold fast in winter quarters, neither deteriorating weather nor supply problems favoured offensive action.

Re-supply was indeed proving difficult. Colonel Guildford Slingsby was defeated and killed by Cholmley at Guisborough on 16 January 1643, Cholmley then bested in turn by the King at Yarm barely a fortnight later. Providing for the Queen remained Newcastle's primary mission. In the event, she made landfall not on the Tyne but at Bridlington, enabling the earl to keep his forces in the county. Though her disembarkation was made lively by Parliamentarian ships from the Royal Navy, Newcastle came up in a timely manner to facilitate the unloading and transport into York of the Royal personage and her equally precious cargo. Newcastle was able to retain some of these much-needed munitions to equip his own forces, whilst the bulk could be sent on to Oxford. At this point, Sir Hugh Cholmley experienced a change of heart, opening the gates of Scarborough. This was bad. Even worse, Lord Fairfax was having doubts about the Hothams and the security of Hull, a major prize for either faction. As the Parliamentarians withdrew towards Leeds, Sir Thomas maintained a rearguard at Tadcaster. As he in turn fell back over Bramham Moor, scene of an earlier fifteenth-century battle where the 1st Earl of Northumberland fell, his over-extended forces were harassed and badly mauled by Goring's cavalry.

Having done his duty by the Queen and with the Fairfaxes retreating, Newcastle could pick up the gauntlet and carry the fight into the West Riding. Though Leeds remained formidable, Wakefield, Rotheram and then Sheffield were all successfully occupied. Strategically these manufacturing towns were a significant boost to the Royalist war economy, but Sir Thomas Fairfax was not minded to sit idle and decided to launch a spoiling raid against Wakefield's garrison on 21 May. A brisk and confused action followed, lively enough as Goring's troopers fought back but Fairfax took the day and with his victory, a rich haul of prisoners and supplies, Goring himself foremost amongst the captives. Newcastle was hamstrung, partially by his own caution and in part by his continuing need to ensure that vital munitions reached Oxford. It was not until the latter part of June that the Royalists got moving again, some initial successes were offset by adverse weather that wet summer and it was not until the 30th that the Royalists began their advance upon their immediate goal – Bradford.

Having decided that their tactical position overall was a weak one the Fairfaxes, despite being outnumbered, decided upon a pre-emptive strike which brought the two armies face-to-face on 30 June at Adwalton Moor – the largest battle in the north after Marston Moor the following year[6]. Despite a dogged resistance by the Parliamentary foot, the day finally and overwhelmingly went to Newcastle, whose army killed perhaps 500 of their foes and took 1,400 prisoners[7].

Sir Thomas and less than 1,000 survivors rallied to hold Bradford, whilst his less aggressive father slipped back into Leeds. Ill-luck dogged the battered Roundheads. The Hothams were now deep into a decisive defection[8] which would have delivered Hull. Tom Fairfax came to grief when he attempted to break through the tightening ring around Bradford. Most of those who'd survived the battle were slain or taken. Leeds proved an illusory sanctuary for the Parliamentarian grip was rapidly unravelling along with Lord Fairfax' nerve; Hull seemed the only safe haven and this was not reached without further scrapping through the streets of Selby, where Sir Thomas suffered a gunshot wound to his left wrist[9]. The Earl of Newcastle's triumph in the north appeared complete[10].

Guarding the Trent

Since December 1642, a Royalist garrison had held Newark sandwiched between Parliament's forces garrisoning Nottingham and Lincoln. In the same month, the Roundhead Midlands and Eastern Associations had been conceived. For some months the Royalists in Newark were left unmolested and given time to work upon their defences. Towards the latter part of February, after some initial skirmishing, the town was invested. Although the works were of limited strength, an initial, rather haphazard, assault was thrown back. The siege ended in a rather ignominious and acrimonious retreat, leaving Newcastle free to send mounted reinforcement. The Royalists sallied out in some style, taking Grantham and beating Hotham and Lord Willoughby of Parham. Colonel Oliver Cromwell was, meanwhile, in charge of detachments of the new Eastern Association's raw formations.

The future Lord Protector began some tentative moves and joined forces with Hotham and Lord Willoughby's remnants at Sleaford on 9 May. Two days later, the Parliamentarians were surprised by energetic Royalists who launched a well-planned spoiling raid. Oliver Cromwell's energy and dash prevented a defeat but support received from his fellow Parliamentarians was at best discouraging. Dissentions between these local commanders frustrated any opportunity Parliament might have had to interrupt the Queen's southward march. Cromwell was beginning, rightly, to be suspicious of Hotham, whose duplicity was soon proven[11]. This hiatus allowed the Queen an uninterrupted passage.

As Parliament's officers bickered, the Newarkers launched a fresh sally, secured Stamford but failed at Peterborough. Lord Willoughby, attempting to restore some semblance of morale, did succeed in taking Gainsborough. Matters for Parliament were at a poor pass. In the west, General Waller ('William the Conqueror') had been conquered himself at Roundway Down[12] and Bristol was threatened. Essex army was enfeebled by disease and urgently in need of replacements. Cromwell had moved against Stamford and then Burghley House, whilst the Royalists were exerting themselves to relieve the Midlanders and Eastern Association of Gainsborough. On 28 July, a sharp engagement was fought outside the town when Cromwell and Sir John Meldrum won a signal victory. Any celebration would have been premature for as the Roundheads, flushed with success, sallied out to take on what they imagined were Royalist survivors or rearguard they stumbled onto a much larger force; Newcastle was marching south.

Once again Gainsborough, so brilliantly won, had to be surrendered whilst Meldrum and Cromwell fell back through Lincoln. The arrival of Newcastle with all his power had significantly altered the balance and the less hardened Roundheads were soon slipping away in droves[13]. Newcastle's march was not necessarily inexorable, far from it. The further south he went, the more his own independent authority evaporated. Stuart Reid[14] is clearly of the opinion that fresh alarums in Yorkshire provided the perfect screen for a pause. Undismayed by their defeat, the Fairfaxes, at least Sir Thomas, had been consolidating behind the walls of Hull and had rebuilt their available forces to a respectable level. Now began something of a see saw; a determined sally by Sir Thomas provided the excuse for Newcastle to turn his forces around and drive the Parliamentarians back behind Hull's defences. To counter the Royalist's attempts at a close leaguer, Fairfax broke down the sluices, creating a floodplain acting as a gigantic moat. From now on Newcastle could only hope to blockade the place but, though re-supply by sea was possible, the large garrison and rump of Fairfax' field army consumed supplies at a prodigious rate.

One significant effect of Newcastle's successes was to boost the role of the Eastern Association. Hitherto, this had been seen as little more than a recruiting mechanism to feed men into Essex army. Now the priority shifted[15] and the Earl of Manchester was commissioned to lead a much larger force which would form a new and largely independent field command[16]. Issuing ordinances and putting 'boots on the ground' were of course two very different matters and the process was hindered by a Royalist reaction in King's Lynn which required a siege to suppress.

By 26 February Fairfax's cavalry, mere *bouche inutiles*★ within the walls, broke out and joined forces with Manchester. By early October the Parliamentarians could muster perhaps 6,000 foot and dragoons with some 1,500 horse[17]. Their planned deployment was to sit down before the walls of Bolingbroke Castle, something of a sledgehammer to crack the proverbial walnut but the Royalists obliged by sending an *ad hoc* force, mainly mounted to relieve the beleaguered garrison. Given the long odds, this was unwise and yet the Cavaliers advanced boldly to contact which occurred at Winceby on 11 October[18]. A very brisk action ensued where the outnumbered Royalists gave a good account of themselves until Fairfax delivered a neat flanking movement and rolled up his enemy's line.

The 11 October was an eventful day for Sir John Meldrum, together with Lord Fairfax, mounted a determined sally upon the besiegers' lines before Hull. The Roundheads were driven off by an equally spirited riposte but steadied, rallied and came on again finally wresting one of the forts from Newcastle's forces. This stroke completed the creeping decline in the besiegers' morale and the Royalists abandoned their waterlogged trenches to fall back upon York. Meldrum broke free and re-took both Lincoln and Gainsborough – Newark was again isolated. Newcastle dithered, choosing to begin a rather pointless excursion into Derbyshire as the campaigning season drew to a close.

★ An expression from the Hundred Years War – 'useless mouths'.

Raising the Stakes

By the end of 1643, neither side could claim to have secured a decisive advantage. The north was generally still held for the King, though Newcastle's grip was far from certain and the threat of a Scottish invasion would tilt the balance quite dramatically as the marquis (as he now was) could scarcely contain the Yorkshire Parliamentarians with their Eastern Association allies on the one hand and counter the Scots on the other. For Sir Thomas Fairfax there was to be no respite after his re-taking of Gainsborough on 20 December. He was thereafter assigned to facilitate the relief of Nantwich. Throughout 1643 the war had sparked and flared in the north-west. With the spectre of a Scots army descending upon the north, Charles had, in September, brokered a truce with the Irish rebels. This did not end hostilities on that side of the Irish Sea but it did have the effect of releasing significant forces from Royalist contingents in Leinster and Munster[19].

This was, for Parliament, a most serious development. The spectre of thousands of Royalist reinforcements pouring in through the western ports was truly frightful. In propaganda terms, however, it was a veritable godsend, for the pamphleteers could howl out dire predictions of rapine and horror as this vast Papist horde descended. Whilst Charles might have favoured a mass landing of his Irish regiments, circumstances did not favour such a grand and undoubtedly impressive gesture. Rather, the Duke of Ormonde, Charles' commander in Ireland was constrained to ship as many across as the available shipping could carry. Some landed in Bristol[20] and some at Whitehaven but Chester offered by far the best prospects as a port of entry.

Sir Thomas Fairfax commanded perhaps 2,500–3,000 foot, 500 dragoons and some 1,800 horse. His Royalist opponent, Lord Byron had perhaps a similar number of infantry but far less cavalry and dragoons. The battle of Nantwich, fought on 25 January resulted in a decisive Parliamentarian victory[21]. This wrested control of the north-west away from the King, and greatly enhanced Fairfax' rising star – a phenomenon which would ultimately be crowned by full command of all Roundhead forces with the formation of the New Model Army in 1645. Royalist losses in the fight, perhaps 200 dead, were not severe, but a further 1,500 were taken along with a quantity of guns and most of Byron's baggage[22]. Most importantly, the virtual Royalist hegemony in the north-west was irretrievably broken.

For the King this was a rather poor beginning to 1644. Though defeated, Byron clung onto Chester and a nucleus of Irish regiments had been successfully landed, sufficient to form the makings of a cohesive force being mustered at Shrewsbury. These forces were then formed into the core of a mobile field army to be commanded by Rupert who had assumed command in Shrewsbury by 19 February[23]. With characteristic élan, the prince routed a Parliamentarian force barring his path at Market Drayton and proceeded to rendezvous with Byron at Chester. Now, however, a fresh threat arose to the isolated but crucial outpost of Newark. Newcastle appears to have lost sight of this vital bastion and the fact that Meldrum was steadily gaining ground in Lincolnshire whilst the marquis pursued a rather ephemeral campaign in Derbyshire.

The marquis' inertia allowed Meldrum to close the ring around Newark. There was no attempt to push home an escalade and repeat the debacle of the previous year. A rather feeble and fore-doomed attempt with inferior forces to break the ring foundered and it was left to Rupert to mount a sizeable relief. Never one to shirk a challenge, he responded with customary gusto, taking his slender forces from Shrewsbury and picking up such reinforcements as could be pulled together. This *ad hoc* arrangement finally collected some 3,000 foot and as many horse, not all of proven capabilities. A seesaw battle around the Newark lines followed. Rupert behaved with all of his usual bravura but Meldrum put up a solid fight clinging to his works till his forces began to fragment and finally broke, some in open mutiny. His men marched out of their lines on most favourable terms, maintaining their drums and banners, leaving only their personal firearms and ordnance. Rupert's victory secured Newark and engendered yet another swing towards the Royalists in the region. Both Gainsborough and Lincoln were evacuated though the prince had insufficient men to provide viable garrisons.

By now the Marquis of Newcastle had other priorities. In January the Scots had crossed the Tweed (*see* following chapter), he had thus been obliged to draw off significant forces to counter this threat. Despite this urgency, York could not be left uncovered, by 28 January Colonel John Belasyse had been appointed governor[24]. His task was an unenviable one. The defenders of Hull had resumed their aggressive posturing and Scarborough stood at risk of isolation. At the same time Fairfax was again active in the West Riding. Fearing a pincer movement, Belasyse concentrated his available forces on Selby from where he was able, by 25 March, to take Bradford. By now, Fairfax had Belasyse firmly in his sights and launched an attack on Selby on 11 April. Barricaded in the streets, the Royalists put up a stiff resistance though outnumbered by perhaps two to one[25]. Eventually, as the Roundheads fought their way in, only Belasyse's Horse could cut free. Most of the foot, along with the governor himself and a significant number of officers, laid down their swords. York itself was now imperilled.

The Winter War 1644

Damn it all! All this our South stinks of peace.
You whoreson dog, Papiols, come! Let's to music!
I have no life save when the swords clash.
But ah! When I see the standards gold, vair, purple, opposing
And the broad fields below them turn crimson,
Then howl my heart nigh mad with rejoicing.

'Sestina: Altaforte' Ezra Pound

The transition from the defensive to the offensive is one of the most delicate operations in war.

Napoleon Bonaparte

William Lithgow, a Scottish explorer who accompanied the Scottish army under Leven 'that old, little crooked soldier' and took part in the assault, left a full, if not altogether satisfactory, account of the siege. His is a topographical account with fulsome descriptions of locations and buildings. He describes the city walls as 'having a narrow slit in them, through which they might murther [murder] our soldiers'. He does give a good impression of the difficulties faced by the Scots in that dreadful winter s they struggled across the border 'in a dismal snowie season … knee deep snow and blowing and snowing so vehemently that the guides could with great difficulty know the way, and it was enough for the followers to discern the leaders.'

The Army of the Covenant

Long before Leven's army crossed the Tweed in the snowbound winter of 1644, Parliament had sought through economic measures to diminish Newcastle upon Tyne's enthusiasm, or apparent enthusiasm, for the Royalist cause. This bit both ways of course, damaging the capital in turn; 'the city of London and all the greatest part of this kingdom are like to suffer very deeply in the want of that Commodity [coal] … and which is like to have very dangerous consequence in the influence which it may have upon the necessities of the meaner sort'[1]. Sir John Marley, Newcastle's mayor and Caroline zealot, had other concerns, as the Scots, in the closing weeks of 1643, sought an accommodation whereby the mayor was incited by the earl of Lanark 'to betray the town to oure Generall Leslie'[2].

The Scots chronicler asserts that Marley was temporarily removed from office as a result of his inclining toward these overtures, doubtless accompanied by cash inducement. This is probably no more than wishful thinking, though the London pamphlets were brimful of hopeful tidings that the city had or was about to open its gates to Parliament. There were further optimistic mutterings that Marley and Glemham were already at odds: 'From Newcastle the certaine intelligence is that a great difference hath lately arisen between Sir Thomas Glemham (appointed by the Earle of Newcastle to be governor there) and Sir John Marlow now Major and governour of that Towne'[3].

On a less optimistic and more pragmatic note, the 'Parliament Scout' confirmed that two vessels out of Denmark had gained the Tyne safely, one bringing twenty brass cannon with powder and shot and dragging a merchantman laden with corn as prize. Donald, Lord Reay, of Montrose's affinity, was aboard the munitions ship and remained during the siege[4]. The blockade had been triggered in part by the city's refusal to send much-needed coal to London, there was unquestionably an element of mercantile brinksmanship involved! John Chamberlayne, a seaman from King's Lynn, had provided Parliament with valuable intelligence as to the city's readiness. All knew the Scots must come and only the medieval castle was adequately fortified at this point. Marley had perhaps, 500 militia; Glemham commanded perhaps ten times that number but only half were ready. Nonetheless, supplies were coming in, 150 barrels of powder, 500 muskets and a variety of ordnance[5]. Crucially, Chamberlayne relates that there is disaffection within and much coal wanting a market, hamstrung by the blockade. Two forts the 'Spanish Work' (Tynemouth) and the 'Lower Light Fort' (North Shields) were made ready and controlled entrance to the river[6].

The Campaign in Northumberland

Sir Harry Vane had been one of the commissioners treating on behalf of Parliament with the Scots, no easy matter; negotiations had been long and arduous. Vane and his fellow Englishmen sought nothing beyond a political alliance and military cooperation. The Scots wanted more, a good deal more in fact. The English must enter into the Covenant whereby, on the successful conclusion of hostilities, the established Church would be reformed along Presbyterian lines. The Scots were in a strong position; Parliament needed them rather more than they needed Parliament, now was the time to drive the hardest of bargains. Still, the Covenanters could not find moral cause to fight against their lawful sovereign unless it was for the greater good of advancing their faith. Vane temporised but was obliged to concur. The Scottish intervention was to the Royalists in the north, not merely an incursion by the ancient foe but an attack on the very fabric of Anglicanism.

An initial period of 'Phoney War' came to an end on 19 January when the Scots army crossed the Tweed and the winter campaign in the north began in earnest. The weather was dire, witnessing 'a frost so great (the like whereof we had not seen) that in two nights the river Tweed froze so strong that our army and ammunition, which was at Kelso, marched over the ice, which otherwise could not have come over'. Colonel Francis Anderson, commanding one of Glemham's outposts at Wooler, wrote an urgent report to him the next day:

I shall endeavour to keep my quarters hereabouts, until I receive farther orders from you. I am now drawing my whole Regiment into Wooler, having heard for certain as I was now writing, that a great body of the Enemies Foot, and very many Troopes of Horse advanced over Barwick [Berwick] Bridge yesterday, and were as farre as Haggeston [Haggerston] it is conceived this will forthwith march towards Belforde …[7]

Leven's force was substantial, Terry suggests 18,000 foot, 3,000 horse with perhaps 500–600 dragoons[8] – 'weill armit with field pieces, swadden fedderis, and all ingynis of war necessary'. Stuart Reid believes these totals are exaggerated. He counts fifty-two troops of horse with an average of fifty riders creating a total of 2,600. Of twenty-two foot regiments, most were significantly below strength, Leven commanded 198 'colours' or companies but Reid assumes an average of no more than fifty soldiers per unit; a total of only 9,900. This seems on the low side but if we think of 10,000–11,000 infantry with a maximum of 3,000 cavalry and dragoons we would very likely not be far adrift[9]. By Civil War standards, this was still a most formidable force. Leven appears to have had a quantity of ingenious lightweight twelve pounders (firing a 12lb shot) which could be carried, stripped down on pack animals, whilst the heavier pieces were shipped by sea to Blyth[10].

As the Scots advanced into Northumberland, Glemham received a formal summons from Argyll and Sir William Armyne, preserving the niceties of war and stating the justification of their cause. The Royalist Governor replied politely but evasively. On the 22nd Glemham conferred with the county magnates to consider their options. These were fairly limited; to fight was out of the question, the odds far too heavy, to withdraw and hope for relief seemed best. Hardliners favoured a scorched-earth policy, others preferred to minimise damage to property. If he could not fight, Glemham could breathe defiance in ink which he proceeded to do whilst pulling in his outposts and falling back upon Newcastle itself.

Leven's advance continued unimpeded apart from the harsh winter weather, deep snowdrifts and biting easterlies, which acted as a potent delaying force. On 25 January a sudden thaw set in 'which so swelled the waters, whereof there was not a few in their way, that ofttimes in wading it came to the armpits of the foot …' A correspondent writes that it was intended to reach the Tyne by 27 January and summon the city to submit. At this juncture there was no immediate suggestion of siege operations, the walls would be blockaded and bypassed to facilitate the southward march; 'we have no purpose to stay there, unless it be to seize on the Block-Houses [forts] upon the river, that the Parliament ships may come in safely'[11]. Alnwick was occupied, the garrison on Coquet Island surrendered and some seventy men with their gear taken prisoner. By the 28 January the Scots had gained Morpeth.

By now Newcastle was writing rather peevishly to Rupert that he had insufficient resources to take on the Covenanters; 'truly I cannot match five thousand foot, and the horse not well armed. The Scots advanced as far as Morpeth, and they are fourteen thousand as the report goes'[12]. Newcastle's report on numbers would tend to support Reid's view over Terry's. Glemham had broken down a number of bridges, though the artisans he had entrusted with the job of slighting Felton Bridge panicked or were panicked by the entreaties of their wives and bolted[13].

Leven marched out of Morpeth on 1 February intending to plant his standards 'within two miles' of the city by next day. He was, however, impeded by logistical matters and this welcome hiatus permitted the Marquis of Newcastle, hurrying north from York, to get his forces into Newcastle just hours ahead of the Scots. General King wrote to his Sovereign on the 13th, giving an account of the Royalists marches and an upbeat assessment of the overall state of preparedness, having; 'found the town in a very good posture, and that the Mayor, who had charge of it, had performed his part in your majesty's service very faithfully; and all the aldermen and best of the town well disposed for your service'[14].

Before the Walls

King reports a sharp exchange between the trained bands and the advancing Scots before the gates, with the invaders seen off. Sir William Armyne, writing from Morpeth, broadly confirms this:

> The Marquess of Newcastle … came late into the town the night before, which was unknown to us, and upon the approach of some of our soldiers to a work of theirs without the town – where some few were slain – they within set on fire and burnt down all the streets and houses lying without the walls on the north side of the town, by which and other circumstances we gather they are resolved obstinately to hold it out to the last[15].

Any optimism either amongst Covenanters or Parliamentarians that the keys to Newcastle might simply be handed over were fully disappointed, the place would not fall without a fight or protracted siege, neither of which was on Leven's immediate agenda.

Just before the skirmish, the Scots' Commissioners had sent a herald with a conciliatory appeal to the townspeople to open their gates, stressing their intentions and martial appearance were not directed against them and which 'may occasion strange thoughts in you'. By then the first shots had already been fired and 'strange' thoughts were very much order of the day. Marley sent a formal reply, stressing that the burgesses were not about to abandon their allegiance to Charles I and reminding their enemies that Newcastle's army was now within and ready to man the walls[16]. The 'True Relation'[17] gives a fuller account of the attempted escalade:

> Some of our men were drawn up to a stone bridge [over Pandon Burn] a quarter of a mile from the town, at the entrance to the Shield-field to beat out some men of theirs out of a little sconce that lay near it [an unfinished work not to be confused with the Shieldfield fort proper], and did it presently without loss; butt he retired to a sharper work near the Windmill [the Shieldfield Fort], where the controversie was more hot, and our arguments not strong enough … In six hours assault or thereabouts, wee lost only fourteen men. The enemy having about seven or eight, fled to the Town and we possessed the Fort, which is within halfe-musket shot of the walls[18].

Apparently worsted, the defenders now mounted a sally by eight troops of cavalry and the Scots sent in five of their own. The ground was very much an industrial landscape, a veritable warren of open-cast pits which vastly restricted the effective use of mounted troops, 'they could not charge above three in breast together in respect of the Coale-Pits'. The cavalry action saw much popping of pistols but no serious hurt. Two Royalists were captured, one, an officer, 'cursed and railed for halfe an houre together'. That night guns boomed from the ramparts, more a show of defiance than with any tactical purpose. As the outlying dwellings burned, 'we heard the cry of the poor people and it is like to be heard higher'. Leven's official dispatch confirms the action, providing additional details – the attack was made by commanded bodies of shot assaulting from both east and west and that the fight continued till midnight; the Scots officially admitted to the loss of a single officer, a Captain English serving with Lindsay's Regiment and nine other ranks[19].

With the fort lost, Marley now torched the easterly suburbs by Sandgate as he had earlier wasted those lying to the north, a giant blaze which consumed the jumble of timber-framed dwellings and shanties, 'burning all night, and Sunday and Monday all day'. Leven was probably wrong-footed, though his men grabbed whatever shipping lay by Sandgate, there was no sign of collapse. Terry certainly takes the view that his easy victory in 1640 had lulled him into underestimating the resolve of the defenders. Neither Marley nor Newcastle looked set to capitulate and all the heavier Scots guns were still on the seas. Parliament had already attempted to raise fresh funds to underwrite the siege, loans were offered at 8 per cent, a highly attractive offer!

By Tuesday 6 February the ordnance had arrived safely and was dragged to the main Scottish camp. It was Leven's intention to throw a pontoon bridge across the Tyne and thereby net the ships at anchor on the Gateshead side (their escape frustrated by a Parliamentarian squadron lying off the river mouth). This move would also secure coal resources on the south bank and begin an effective blockade of the city. Probably on Friday 11th, the defenders at Tynemouth attempted a sally, sending out a company of musketeers who were worsted and beaten up by Scottish horse, some fourteen of fifteen were killed and around fifty captured. The bulk of these were paroled and returned to Marley, who repaid the courtesy by releasing some Scottish prisoners and 'thanked Leven for his courtesy and expressed the hope that shortly he might be in a position to repay it'[20].

The Marquis of Newcastle wrote a frank appraisal to Charles I which neatly sums up the overall strategic situation:

> … the seat of the war will be in the north, a great army about Newark behind us, and the great Scotch army before us, and Sir Thomas Fairfax very strong for the West Riding of Yorkshire, as they say, and his father master of the East Riding; so we are belet [surrounded] not able to encounter the Scots, and shall not be able to make our retreat for the army behind us. This is the greatest truth of the state of your majesty's affairs, whatsoever any courtier says to the contrary. If your Majesty beat the Scots your game is absolutely won; which can be no other way but by sending more forces, especially foot[21].

Alarums and Excursions

This is a pretty fair assessment and the marquis' logic is difficult to fault. As to what he himself intended, his wife, in her biography, advances the view that he intended to mount a night attack in force against the Scottish camp. Darkly, she hints that any such attempt was thwarted by treasonable divisions within. She mentions no names but suspicion must fall on the Scottish officers, a number of whom were serving but whose loyalties were now suspect: 'there was so much treachery, juggling and falsehood in my Lord's own army, that it was impossible for him to be successful in his designs and undertakings'[22]. This may very possibly be true; equally, it might just be an effective smokescreen to cover Newcastle's indecision. At the best of times a night attack upon enemy quarters was a high-risk venture, not one to be undertaken lightly and where the consequences of failure were likely to be severe. An attack upon the Scottish cavalry outposts offered far more scope for local success.

Sir Marmaduke Langdale and Colonel Fenwick commanded some twenty-five troops of horse with around 400 shot at Hexham. The Scottish outpost at Corbridge, barely 6 miles east, was attacked on the morning of 19 February. The Scottish officers, Leven's son Lord Balgonie and Lord Kirkcudbright were vigilant and drew their men up west of their billet to receive the Royalists. According to the Scots version, Lieutenant Colonel Ballantyne delivered a spirited charge, followed by another and then a third, which drove the Royalist horse back upon their own foot, netting a hundred prisoners. Fenwick's shot, however, saw off Ballantyne's horse and seem to have sent the Covenanters 'reeling in that disorder'. Langdale had planned a pincer attack, detailing Colonel Robert Brandling (with ten mounted troops) to swing around the south bank of the Tyne, through Dilston and so come upon the Covenanters from the rear. The Scots, if finally worsted, retreated in good order and without effective pursuit. Brandling was on his own and found himself facing the whole of Balgonie's force. Undeterred or perhaps to put heart into his troopers, he spurred forward and swapped shots with a Lieutenant Elliot. As the duellists drew swords, the Englishman's horse stumbled; he was thrown or pulled off by his opponent and captured[23]. For the Scots this was overall, a narrow escape, 'I trust it will make us more watchful and confident in God'.

The effect upon morale for both sides was as might be expected; the Cavaliers withdrew in some disorder and the Scots were left in possession of the field. Allowing for the natural bias of the Scottish writer, the affair seems to have concluded as a draw with relatively minor loss on both sides. Newcastle's dispatch to the King, dated 9 March, provides a rather more positive 'spin'. He claims 200 Scottish casualties and 150 prisoners[24]. Balgonie, the marquis asserts, was wounded and taken as were three colours, two cavalry and one dragoon. Colonel Douglas from Prudhoe also sallied out to beat up the Covenanters' quarters at Prudhoe, driving in all their outposts in that vicinity.

The Sunderland Campaign

Whilst such aggression was commendable, Newcastle lacked sufficient numbers to see the Covenanters off and there was no real possibility of keeping them penned on the north bank of the Tyne. On 22 February Leven resolved to resume his southward progress. Leaving six regiments of foot (Mearns and Aberdeen, the Strathearn, the 'Levied' Battalion, The Merse, Nithsdale and Annandale regiments), together with a commanded body of horse under Sir James Lumsden, he marched out with the rest. A Scottish correspondent describes their advance:

We marched from our Quarters near Newcastle to Hedden on the Wall, some four miles
up the river; and all that night lay in the fields, almost in the very same place where we
quartered the night before our crossing Tyne at Newburn in the last expedition; which
passage the enemy had now fortified, not only upon the river side, but above neer the top
of the hill…Upon the 23 day, we marched forward and were quartered along the river side
from Ovingham to Corbridge, about two miles distant from Hexham: Whereupon the
other side appeared some of the enemies Horse marching toward us; but about midnight,
their Regiments of Horse that were at Hexham marched thence …Upon Wednesday the
28, we passed Tyne, without any opposition, at three several fords …[25].

The sluggish, cold waters of Tyne were much swollen by melting snow and the foot waded
thigh deep in icy waters, for a week the levels had been too high to allow infantry to pass over
safely. Their next river obstacle was the Derwent, also flowing full. Fording here was out of
the question and the men had to file across a makeshift bridge at Ebchester, camping in the
cold, sodden winter fields. Leven's objective was the town and port of Sunderland and the
Scots reached Chester-le-Street on 1 March. 'The day was very cold, and in the afternoon
came on a thick rainy mist'. Though Newcastle's scouts were shadowing the Scottish host,
there was no attempt at interdiction. By 4 March the Covenanters had reached Wearside
and entered the town unopposed, if distinctly unwelcome. The thorny business of re-supply
proved taxing; 'All that day and the day following was spent in taking care to supply the Army
with Provisions, which we obtained with no small difficulty, being the enemies Country'[26].

Newcastle had, as the Scots settled into occupation of Sunderland, been drawing in
reinforcements, trained bands from Durham and a further dozen troops of the Northern
Horse under Sir Charles Lucas. The stripping of such few provisions as might be remaining
by the Scots and the region's dependence upon the city of Newcastle as an importer
of grain would have had a severe effect upon the populace. In the early afternoon of
6 March, his forces tramped over that same bridge across the Wear that had witnessed the
Scots passage four days earlier. Scottish vedettes watched from atop Penshaw Hill (where
the monument now stands), some scrimmaging followed and, next days, both armies drew
up in battle order. The weather had again turned wintry and snow, in copious quantities,
was falling. That same Scottish correspondent takes up the story:

Upon Thursday the 7, the enemy drew up their Forces upon a height about two short miles
from us; but the snow fell in such abundance, that nothing could be done till the middle of the
day, that it was fair; at which time we advanced towards them, and they marched northwards,
as is conceived to gain the wind. Both armies were drawn up in Battle, the enemy having
the advantage of the ground; but we could not without very great disadvantage engage our
Army, in regard of the impassable ditches and hedges between us …[27].

Stuart Reid, quite rightly I feel, places the Scots at this juncture upon Humbledon Hill
and the Royalists on Penshsw. The narrow valley of the Barnes Burn, doubtless in spate,
also impeded any attempts to engage. The Scots held the field that evening 'in a very
cold night' before advancing again next morning[28]. That day, the 8th, proved somewhat
livelier. Mounted vedettes 'skirmished wherein the advantage that was, fell upon our

side'. As the Scottish foot advanced, the Royalists continued to fall back. The Scottish correspondent gives Newcastle a total strength of 14,000 but this must be far too high, the northern English were very likely significantly outnumbered. Newcastle had previously complained of inadequate forces, the campaigning in the north thus far would have taken its toll, desertion and sickness would account for more. As they retreated they burned cottages and bothies creating a dense shroud of smoke.

As Leven's skirmishers gained the crest of Penshaw, the Scots prepared to smite Newcastle's rearguard but the weather, once again, disobliged. Under cover of this providential snowstorm, Newcastle marched for Durham. The Scottish writer believed 'they have suffered great loss, many of their men and horse dying, but more run away; we hear they have lost of their Horse 800 besides the loss of their foot'[29]. Both sides had suffered from the dismal cold and it may well be the local side lost more, many faint-hearts might use the pall of snow to cover a discreet exit.

Leven had other problems, which the Scottish correspondent admits. Supply was proving a major headache. Those provisions which could be requisitioned or bought were fast disappearing into the army's hungry maw. Five supply vessels had attempted to beat down the east coast but three were lost and the others driven into the Tyne where they were joyfully seized. The cavaliers had wasted the country and driven off anything on legs 'so that sometimes the whole Army hath been ready to starve, having neither meat nor drink'. On the 12th an advance toward Durham began, again unopposed but was abandoned for fear the port might be attacked and attention switched to the Royalist outpost at South Shields. Writing in a further dispatch, the same correspondent takes up the narrative:

> On the 15, at night a party was commanded out to assault the Fort upon the South side Tine over against Tinemouth Castle, which they did but with no success, though with little loss; after we had considered of this repulse two or three days and fasted on the nineteenth, the Fort was again assaulted by another party; for the encouragement of which the General went with them in person, and on the 20, being Wednesday in the morning we took it with the loss of nine men, the hurt of more[30].

The Scots netted a haul of five iron guns, seven barrels of powder and some seventy small arms. Most of the garrison escaped across the river; only a small rearguard comprising a lieutenant and half a dozen men, were captured. A contemporary pamphlet, *The Taking of the Fort at South Shields*[31], provides more detail of the successful attack.

Colonels Stewart and Lyell, Lieutenant Colonels Bruce and Johnston led the assault – men drawn from the Linlithgow, Tweeddale and Stirlingshire regiments. The fort was strong, a deep ditch and wide, high ramparts beyond, shielded in part by the castle guns over the water. A Royalist man-o-war added more firepower. The commanded party, 140 strong, advanced steadily under fire, using bundles of sticks or withies to bridge the fosse. Once this obstacle was overcome, both pike and shot attempted to storm the redoubt. The fight was long and hotly contested. Despite the defenders' barrage, Scots soldiers clawed their way in through the exposed gun ports and mounted scaling ladders. Once they'd gained a foothold, the cavaliers' resolve evaporated and the fort fell. The pamphleteer claims that sixteen were left behind dead[32].

An English writer, William Tunstall in correspondence with his father-in-law Sir Edward Radcliffe, claims that those failed assaults cost the Scots dear: 'Upon the place where they first assaulted it there lay many dead bodies'[33]. Tunstall rather optimistically puts the Covenanter dead as high as 200, and considers the final successful attack cost them another 300! This seems impossibly high and one suspects the figure of say a dozen dead on each side in the last assault to be about right. March 20 proved a good day for Scotland as the energetic Lieutenant Colonel Ballantyne, who had fought earlier at Corbridge, beat up Royalist quarters at Chester-le-Street and took two score prisoners. Storming the fort at South Shields was not just a tactical victory; it vastly improved the Scots supply position for their foothold on the south side enabled them to plunder prizes seeking the haven. Thus far, Leven, if he had failed to browbeat the Newcastle burgesses into submission, had gained control over most of Northumberland and North Durham. Sunderland, if a good deal smaller, was still a viable port.

Strategically, if the Marquis of Newcastle had failed to drive off the Scots and, given his slender resources this was never likely, he had at least kept the Royal standard flying over the city and his army in being, undefeated in the field. His scorched-earth policy and the vile winter weather had left the Scots in not inconsiderable difficulties. The defenders were still proactive, 'biffing' the enemy; there is suggestion of a skirmish at Elswick on 14 March[34]. Leven was by now considering his further advance, hoping that the more hospitable pastures of Yorkshire might offer greater sustenance. He would also hope to join forces with the Parliamentarians so very active there. Such a union could only be disastrous for King Charles.

The mercurial and brilliant Montrose had reached Durham on 15 March to join forces with the marquis. He had little to offer in the way of reinforcement, but his dynamism had a marked effect upon the older and far more cautious general. He had hoped Newcastle could supply him with an adequate force to commence operations 'having some design for the King's cause in Scotland … and although the marquis could not conveniently spare any, having so great an army to oppose, yet to advance his Majesty's service as much as lay in his power, he lent Montrose 200 horse and dragoons'. On 23 March the Royalists marched resolutely from Durham towards Chester-le-Street and, next day, took up position atop Boldon Hill on the north bank of the Wear. Leven conformed, his forces deployed to the east of their enemies along Whitburn Lizard. The two armies were now some 3 miles distant[35].

Leven's difficulties were compounded by the fact his ordnance was still within Sunderland and he relied upon sailors to transport one great piece over the water. These willing mariners dragged this great gun to the field – most of the rest stayed immured where they were as the tide had retreated. Though an early spring afternoon, both armies faced each other till, 'toward five o'clock' an artillery duel erupted. This was loud if largely ineffective. Next rival outposts clashed amidst contested hedges. The infantry firefight continued in darkness, flashes of fire stabbing through the cloak of the night.

Much powder and shot was expended, though neither side gained much ground. The Scottish correspondent claims his side had rather the better of it, though this may be questionable. Few seem to have died and morning brought stalemate. Stuart Reid takes the view that, allowing for wastage on both sides since the campaign began, they were now pretty evenly matched even if, as we know, Lumsden brought in his cavalry from the blockade[36]. I am less persuaded, we cannot of course be sure, but I tend to suspect Newcastle may have suffered rather more from sickness and desertion, the lure of a warm hearth can be a most attractive one faced with such vile weather and rugged, dangerous campaigning.

The pamphleteer who described the attack on South Shields Fort also gives an account of this action. His version is not dissimilar; he refers to the ground being constricted by hedgerows. If the fight was not as bloody as others it was still hard-fought: 'Many officers who have been old soldiers did affirm they had never seen so long and hot service in the night time.' The Scots account continues in the assertion that the Royalists suffered more dead and wounded and that some seven wagon-loads of wounded were evacuated from the field. Not unsurprisingly, the Royalist telling differed somewhat and the report which appeared in *Mercurius Aulicus*[37] painted a more favourable canvas:

> The fight began about three in the afternoon and continued from that time until night, and continued more or less till next morning … next morning (being Monday) the Lord Marquis followed them till afternoon, and then they vanished instantly into their trenches and retirement in Sunderland.

This can easily be viewed as a somewhat rose-tinted view, spin in the modern sense. Newcastle was simply not strong enough to drive the Scots back into Sunderland and almost certainly it was he who was on the back-foot and obliged to withdraw. *Mercurius Aulicus* claims 1,000 Scottish casualties and admits to the loss of 240 of the marquis' men. This was then a rather larger affair than has been previously considered the case; the Scots had expended no less than thirty-seven barrels of powder[38]. The Marquis of Newcastle's retreat was covered by Sir Charles Lucas' cavalry. By 26 March the Cavaliers were back in Durham.

The March into Yorkshire

A brief hiatus now ensued whilst Leven made his further preparations. He appears to have been in no particular hurry; time, in a number of ways time was on his side and spring was driving back those residual tentacles of winter. On 31 March the Covenanters marched westwards from Sunderland. Newcastle did not contest their advance and, on 12 April, abandoned Durham and withdrew further south. It appears that, as the Royalists marched towards Bishop Auckland, it was the marquis' intention to hold the line of the Tees[39]. Once news of the debacle at Selby was brought, probably at Barnard Castle on the 13th[40], then there was no other choice but to abandon the north-east and march directly for York before Fairfax' victorious forces could scoop this most valuable of prizes. York was the northern capital. Its loss would have been a disaster of the first magnitude.

There had been some criticism that Leven, for all his grand reputation and undoubted achievement, was becoming rather too aged for such active campaigning and that his best days now lay behind him[41]. Nonetheless, as Stuart Reid very rightly points out, his decision to effectively abandon all gains in the north-east and pursue the Marquis of Newcastle was strategically crucial and indeed eminently sound. He had rightly divined that the key to success in the north lay not so much in the capture of the city of Newcastle but in the elimination of the marquis' field army, whereby all other prizes would fall like ripe plums.

A Scottish correspondent, John Somerville, quartermaster to Eglinton's Horse, takes up the account of the pursuit which now ensued:

And upon the 12th in the night, the Marquis of Newcastle with his army fled from Durham; and we got no intelligence till the 13th at three o'clock in the afternoon and then the army marched after them with all the haste they could, but they had got a head start and we came to Ferryhill that night; and on the 14th, being a Sunday we marched very early, before the sun rose, and the horsemen followed in haste and came to Darlington before seven o'clock in the morning and sent out a party of horse to pursue their rear[42].

Such energy paid dividends. The Scottish horse caught up with stragglers and beat up Newcastle's rearguard, 'took forty men and many horses and slew many of their stragglers and got two thousand marks worth of sliver plate …' The Scots passed the Tees unopposed and advanced to Northallerton and, on the 16th from there to Thormanby, then on to Boroughbridge and on the 16th joined forces with Fairfax at Wetherby. Newcastle had reached uncertain sanctuary behind the walls of York, his cavalry under Langdale was sent off to join the King whilst he settled down with the remnants of foot to endure a siege. Another Scottish correspondent[43] assumed these manoeuvres and the bottling up of Newcastle's army in York heralded the end of campaigning in Durham and Northumberland: 'we now have free liberty to make use of all the coals upon the River Wear, and are in good hopes of those upon the River Tyne very shortly when out army is at leisure to demand Newcastle, whose garrison is almost exhausted.' Stripped of the marquis' army, the defence of the city would indeed look rather thin but with the Scots army bogged down before York the forces left behind were themselves inadequate to capitalise on the Royalists' weakness.

Montrose, at this point viewed by his Cavalier contemporaries as a somewhat quixotic figure, had fought in the earlier fight at Hilton but had subsequently been permitted, as mentioned, to take Sir Robert Clavering and a company of horse to investigate Royalist prospects in the south-west of Scotland. These proved rather less than promising and by mid-April he had returned to Northumberland. The Scottish marquis displayed his customary energy and, around 10 May, together with Lord Crawford, he attacked the Parliamentary outpost at Morpeth.

Here the garrison was stoutly defended by captains Somerville and McCulloch, who beat off a first attempt and obliged the Royalists to wait for the arrival of half a dozen guns from Newcastle. The siege continued briskly for nearly three weeks until the garrison struck their colours on 29 May; an attempt by Scottish horse to break the ring was seen off. For the Cavaliers their butcher's bill was a high one; a major, three captains, a further trio of lieutenants, four ensigns and 180 other ranks had fallen[44], a high price for so modest a gain.

Montrose now went on to recover the fort at South Shields which the Scots commander, Rutherford of Ranfurly, appears to have sold out and for which deceit the turncoat was subsequently court-martialled[45]. A similar design was then launched to recover the larger prize of Sunderland and some suborning of the garrison may have been attempted. In any event, a body of mariners, more determinedly disposed towards Parliament, took control of the defences, manned their guns and, with the aid of Colonel Charles Fairfax, saw off

A typical musketeer of the 1640s (notice the absence of body armour). He is carrying a matchlock and set of 'apostles'.

Detail of a recreated matchlock mechanism, showing the pan cover and jaws with match in place.

Above left: A recreated Lochaber axe, a broad elliptical blade on plain ash staff.

Above right: Recreated cavalry backswords, note only the leading edge is sharpened; this was a very cost efficient means of producing a serviceable blade.

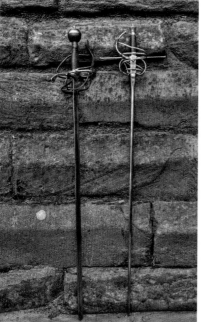

Recreated civilian rapiers, thin long-bladed weapon intended primarily for the thrust.

Right: The Black Gate, Newcastle's barbican (arguably). The top two storeys were added in the early seventeenth century.

Below: Recreated female civilian everyday wear. Women who followed the armies of the Civil War might have looked like this.

Left & below: The Chapel in the Keep; views of nave and chancel and the fine Norman detail which is still intact.

Right: A model of the Castle as it might have appeared in the High Middle Ages and showing its location upon the plateau, a view now much distorted by the subsequent railway construction.

Below: Internal displays in the lower hall area, improvised bills and a portrait of Sir John Marley.

The internal stairway leading to the upper gallery and roof of the keep.

Civil War graffiti in the King's Chamber.

The south elevation of the Norman keep with subsequent repairs including the intact fore-building, unique apart from that at Dover and probably executed by the same hand.

A remarkably intact section of curtain wall along Orchard Street, south of the railway.

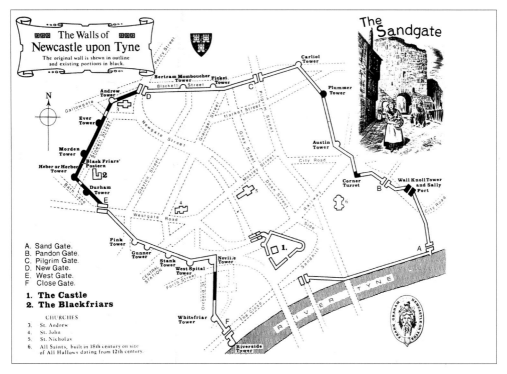

The Campaign of 1644, January–April.

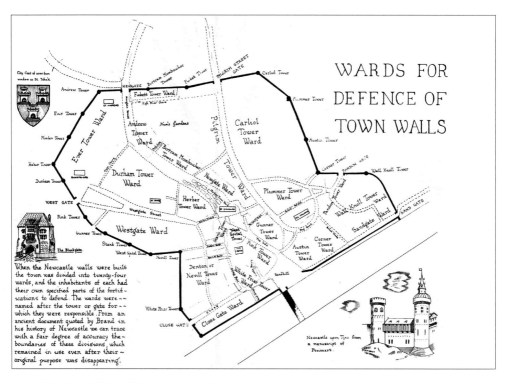

The Town Walls of Newcastle upon Tyne in 1644.

the attempt[46]. It was now some five months since the great Scottish army had crossed the Tweed in dead of winter. Since then, Parliamentary hopes of a swift capture of Newcastle had largely evaporated. Montrose had injected a measure of aggression into the garrison whose active defence had heavily eroded gains already won. On 25 June, a further Scottish force under the Earl of Callendar had marched south. For Leven's officers this was none too soon for they had seen how their position had deteriorated.

In May, Lord Lindsay had written to the Commissioners from before the walls of York:

We entreat your lordships not to delay in sending these forces [Callendar] into England; for if it had been done in time, a few horsemen with our foot forces here and Colonel Weldon's regiment, might have been more than sufficient for securing both these counties … and bringing the town of Newcastle to great straits, which we fear shall now become a work of greater difficulty to a stronger power.

General Baillie echoes these sentiments:

The delay of Callendar's in coming so long has given time to the marquis of Newcastle to make havoc [i.e. strip bare] of the northern counties, which will make the Siege of Newcastle the harder[47].

Such gloomy predictions were by no means misplaced. Leven's winter campaign had failed in its expressed primary objective of securing Newcastle, the city remained defiant and the Scottish officers were correct in prophesising it would now be a tough nut to crack. Equally, the Covenanters had driven the Marquis of Newcastle and his field army back into the defences of York where, should he not be relieved his eventual position must become desperate. If York was lost Newcastle's position would become hopeless. For both sides matters now stood at a critical stage.

No Coals from Newcastle – Autumn 1644

The boast of heraldry, the pomp of power,
And all that beauty, all that wealth e'er gave,
Awaits alike th' inevitable hour:-
The paths of glory lead but to the grave.

'Elegy written in a Country Churchyard' Thomas Gray (1716–1771)

When you are occupying a position which the enemy threatens to surround, collect all your force immediately, and menace him with an offensive movement.

Napoleon Bonaparte

The Battle of Marston Moor

On 2 July 1644, not far beyond the shelter of York's ancient walls, the fate of the north was finally decided at Marston Moor, the largest fight in the whole bloody course of the Civil Wars. Rupert had responded to Newcastle's pleas and brought a relief army, perhaps 8,000 strong, swelled by Goring and Lucas with 5,000 horse and a further 800 foot. His orders from the King were ambiguous; he was to relieve the city but was not barred from fighting a general engagement. Given the Prince's martial and aggressive disposition, it was sure he would construe his instructions accordingly. Older courtiers were horrified at the implications.

Moving with customary alacrity, he was at Knaresborough by 30 June. The combined forces of the Scots and Parliamentarians established a blocking position at Long Marston. Rupert neatly sidestepped through Boroughbridge, Overton and Poppleton, captured a pontoon bridge indifferently guarded and entered York on 1 July. He was resolved to give battle, neither Newcastle nor King favoured the idea but reluctantly accepted his order. Newcastle's Tercio, with his Whitecoats was of course present. The Whitecoats, it is said, gained their name from the undyed white wool of their doublets; insufficient dye being available at the time. 'They requested him [Newcastle] to let them have it un-dyed as it was, promising they themselves would dye it in the enemy's blood.'

Consequently, the Allies drew up with Cromwell's horse on their right, assisted by David Leslie, the Anglo-Scottish foot drawn up in three lines, Fairfax and his cavalry on the left. Newcastle's foot formed the bulk of the Royalist centre with Byron and Goring on their flanks. Even with the union of Rupert's and Newcastle's forces those of Parliament still enjoyed a significant numerical superiority. It seemed as the two armies stood, flags flapping in the long drowsy warmth of a summer's afternoon, that no battle would be fought that day. Just before 7 p.m. the guns crashed in a loud if largely ineffective cannonade. Then the foot began to march. Many Royalists had relaxed and were eating their rations thinking the day too far advanced. Goring charged home and routed the Scots opposite. Cromwell's men did rather better, though he was himself wounded. The infantry fight in the centre raged long and hard and indeed it seemed as though Newcastle's foot might yet win a glorious victory and save the north for their King. Cromwell, however, now returned to the field and threw his cavalry against their uncovered flank.

This was the crisis and Cromwell's resolute action decided the battle. Newcastle's Whitecoats formed a courgageous rearguard as the broken Royalists streamed away. Forced into White Syke Close, they sold their lives dearly; few survived. Rupert was obliged to hide in a bean field. The Marquis of Newcastle would never raise such a force again and fled to the Continent. York was lost, with it the north and arguably the war. Charles himself had taken command of his Oxford army and run rings around Essex, forcing him to ignominious surrender in the Lostwithiel campaign. He then went on to trounce Waller at Cropredy Bridge on 29 June but these victories, whilst dazzling, could not compensate for disaster in the north. The city of Newcastle was now more exposed than ever and about to become the front line.

For William Cavendish, Marquis of Newcastle, the man who had held the north for the King, beaten Fairfax, defied Leven, held Newcastle and York, there began seventeen long years of penurious exile, his great fortune dissipated. Like many who suffered much in the service of the Stuarts, gratitude tended to be limited if not altogether lacking. He did not find the restoration Court congenial and retired to his truncated estates in an attempt to salvage what he could. He died at the considerable age of eighty-four:

> He liked the pomp and absolute authority of a general well, and preserved the dignity
> of it to the full; and for the discharge of the outward state and circumstance of it, in acts
> of courtesy, affability, bounty and generosity he abounded, which in the infancy of a war
> became him, and made him for some time very acceptable to men of all conditions[1].

Operations in Northumberland & Durham

With Leven's army bogged down in the siege of York any offensive operations in Northumberland and Durham would have to be undertaken by the reserve forces under Callendar. Rushworth[2] suggests some ten thousand were deployed but Terry[3] favours a lesser figure. Given that most of the available forces had marched with Leven in January, the rump would be considerably less. Moreover, Montrose was about to metamorphose from quixotic chevalier into the bandit-cum-guerrilla of legend[4]. As Callendar traced the footsteps of Leven's army, now marching in easier summer weather, he re-occupied

Morpeth, crossed the Tyne at Newburn and made sure of the Scots bastion at Wearside, still ably held by the seamen who'd seen off the early Royalist attempt. South Shields fort was also back in Scottish hands. On 24 July, Callendar was before Hartlepool which was speedily evacuated under terms by Sir Edmund Carey[5], Stockton also fell. With York's capitulation on 16 July, Leven was free to march north and deal with the unfinished business of Newcastle, his forces and those of Callendar combined would indeed be formidable.

By 7 August, the victors of Marston Moor were marching northwards. The noose was tightening, but the Scots were short of supplies generally and above all of cash. Sir Adam Hepburn and Thomas Hatcher had written to the Estates on 25 July urgently asking for funds: 'whereby that [Callendar's] army may be enabled to prosecute that service while summer lasts, they at present having neither money, clothes, nor means to subsist'[6]. As Leven's army commenced its trek northwards, Callendar was displaying considerable energy – on 27 July he stormed Gateshead.

His subsequent dispatch[7] informs us that he had sent a strong party from Usworth to take Gateshead in a night or dawn attack, but daylight came on and the Royalists sent forces to the high ground of Windmill Hill. Callendar immediately marched his available forces to drive these impudent cavaliers off the high ground and down to the crossings. The Scots now entered into possession of Gateshead which Callendar was confident he could easily hold till Leven came up – the Royalists had no hope of help from any quarter. The defenders were bottled up and Callendar reported only one casualty in the skirmish; 'David Lindsay, who it seems was going over to the enemy – a letter found upon him was written to the Earl of Crawford' [then in Newcastle].

The dour Lithgow comments on the fight for the Windmill Hill:

They were rancountered [encountered] with the enemy at the top of the Windmill Hill where, being prevented by night, and the enemy stronger than they, they were constrained to turn back. Whereupon the next day the Lieutenant General himself came up with the residue of his army and fiercely facing the enemy, beat them from the hill, chased them down the Gatesyde and rushing them along the bridge, closed them within the town[8].

His account of the fight for the Gateshead side tallies neatly with the content of Callendar's official dispatch.

He then goes on to relate how the Scots next contended the bridge itself:

The next day he began to dispute for the enjoying of the bridge, with the fiery service of cannon and musket, which indeed was manfully invaded, and as courageously defended …he [Callendar] gained the better half of the bridge, and with much ado fortified the same with earthen ramparts and artillery … This being regardfully done, he caused to erect five batteries along the Bankhead, and just opposite to the town, from whence the cannon did continually extremely good service, not only against the walls and batteries but also against particular places, and particular persons: Besides the frequent shooting of pot –pieces and other fireworks of great importance which daily annoyed the inhabitants of the town[8].

Tightening the Vice

By this time, a further squadron of ten vessels had sailed to reinforce the blockade and Leven had detached David Leslie with three regiments of horse and one of dragoons to bolster Callendar, who had complained of the slow pace of the main forces in coming to his aid. By 10 August, Leven had reached Bishop Auckland where Callendar and he met. On the 12th the army moved up to Gateshead whilst Leven toured the coastal outposts. That Wednesday, the 14th, the Scots splashed across the slow waters of Tyne at Newburn and occupied Elswick. A siege could now begin in earnest. In summer weather, accommodation for the Scottish troops was not unduly problematic, the men constructed 'huts which they made of turf, clay, straw and wattles, where their halls, chambers, kitchens and cellars are all one'.

Callandar remained unhappy, pointing out in peevish correspondence that Leven's men had benefited from largess in the amount of £4,000, sufficient to relieve all their needs, whilst his own forces remained in dire want. Powder and shot were likewise in demand. It was now becoming clear the reduction of the city would be a rather protracted business. Some time later on 21 August Callendar wrote a further report setting out what was being done to complete encirclement of the city. Typically, he takes the opportunity to complain of a lack of entrenching tools and the continuing dearth of funds. Chamberlain's accounts imply that the besieged were rather better provided for than their adversaries at this stage. Callendar had taken Sinclair's and the Earl Marischall's regiments over the Tyne to establish an eastern bridgehead. He had further constructed a pontoon bridge east of Sandgate. Terry places this east of the Ouseburn, where the topography would provide cover from the defender's guns – using a natural bend in the river and the higher ground between Pandon and Ouseburn[10]. His inspection was harassed by fire from the walls and from Shieldfield fort, which the defenders had again occupied. Terry argues this sconce lay on the east bank of Pandon Burn adjacent New Bridge Street, standing some 550 yards and marginally north of the line of the walls from Carliol Tower[11]. This is broadly in agreement with the current view advanced by John Mabbitt and tallies with the contemporary accounts which refer to 'a fourgates fort'.

The Siege

Leven, in overall command, was tightening the vice. Callendar had extended his original blockade on the Gateshead side to encompass the eastern flank of the city; the two positions linked by an improvised and sheltered crossing. Lithgow states that security of the bridge was entrusted to Kenmure's Regiment, strengthened by a series of three keels, roped together as a form of floating guardhouse. It is likely that the low plateau on which St Ann's now stands formed a fire position for a further gun battery. Mining operations began around Sandgate. Leven was a believer in the efficacy of mining, a tactic as old as warfare itself. As the Scottish guns belched fire, many of the inhabitants living close to the river were driven away from the banks to seek safety.

Lithgow, who is rather vague as to the details of the enveloping operations, does report that Leven had, on the west side and presumably close to Elswick, built a further pontoon bridge, again out of sight of defenders' guns. He does confirm that Leven dug trenches around the west and north-west elevations of the city, almost joining with those excavated by Callendar on the east, only the projecting bastion of Shieldfield fort preventing a complete encirclement. The besiegers themselves settled down to a monotonous and by no means comfortable existence in their improvised bothies whilst officers fared marginally better under canvas in 'circulating [circular] pavillions'.

Regrettably, we do not have a contemporary narrative to inform us of what was happening at this time within the walls. Lithgow does confirm that the streets leading down to the various gates 'were also casten up with defensive breastworks and planted with demi-culverins of iron: And above all other works the Town Castle itself was seriously enlarged, with diverse curious fortifications, besides breast works, redoubts and terreniat demilunes; and withal three distinctive horne-workes, two of which are exteriourly and strongly pallisaded, and of great bounds'[12]. Throwing stones were ready to be hurled from the walls, gaps between merlons filled with rubble and mortar. The gates were firmly closed, propped and barricaded. The external ditch had been cleared and deepened, masonry plastered with a rough mix of slick, puddled clay. Various outbuildings and random structures which had been allowed to obscure the walls and impeded fields of fire were removed[13].

In the usual way, before all of this vast labour had been expended, Leven had on 16 August, summoned the city to surrender 'and your City may reap the sweet fruits of peace, which other Cities under obedience of King and Parliament do quietly enjoy …'[14]. Marley and the council returned an equally courteous response next day, 'if your high respects to his Majesties honour, the shunning of further effusion of blood, the preservation of Newcastle from ruin and extremity of War, be real, return home with your army, live in peace and let your neighbours enjoy the same …'[15].

These high sentiments masked the reality that the Scots were daily strengthening their positions and their inexorable grip which the defenders had neither means nor prospects to disturb. Not all citizens shared Marley's fighting spirit. Several of the less determined aldermen had slipped out and sought sanctuary in Sunderland. Leven had conscripted or hired a significant labour force comprising some 3,000 colliers, keelmen and general labourers. Ironically these were the very classes who had resented digging for the Royalists! Leven appears to have put rather more faith in mining operations than in the efficacy of his great guns. On Saturday 20 August, the defenders sallied out to beat up the besiegers' quarters by Closegate. A couple of Scots were killed and more, including several officers, captured[16].

It was not only faint-hearts within who were revealing low morale. As early as 22 August, two days after the successful sortie, Leven was writing to complain about levels of desertion in his ranks: 'send to the army all such as have run away from their colours and are come home.' That both sides remained active is clear. When the Scottish Chancellor, Lord Loudoun, arrived on a tour of inspection he was treated, on 24 August, to the spectacle of a further sally by the defenders. He had already witnessed intense activity on the part of both besiegers and besieged – the Scots daily extended their works and burrowed furiously whilst the defenders' guns, most particularly those from the castle, kept up a steady barrage. General Baillie was concentrating his efforts against the great bulwark of Newgate, his guns most likely placed on the Leazes from where they inflicted considerable damage, not just upon the enceinte but also on St Andrew's Church.

The Pressure Mounts

Here, by Leazes, mines were also creeping close to the walls and Baillie, having enjoyed his lunch on the 24th, found his digestion disturbed by a sortie in which the besiegers, amongst whom were very few officers, put up a poor showing. Lithgow comments upon such alarums but provides tantalisingly sparse detail: 'So also the inveterate enemy, making now and then diverse sallies from town (issuing at postern gates) upon our flanking trenches, engaged themselves into great jeapordies, and our soldiers to as desperate a defence.'[17] Robert Douglas, a minister who had been with the army since spring, kept a diary during the siege and witnessed these events. He confirms that there was a chronic shortage of officers at this point[18].

The minister delivered a rousing sermon from Leven's base at Elswick that Sunday, hoping spiritual nourishment might offset the lack of more practical assistance from the commissariat. Throughout the siege, snipers remained active. Sharpshooters from both sides, probably employing flint guns as opposed to firelocks, would pick off anyone in range injudicious enough to present a target. One burial entry for 3 September records the interment of 'a man that was shot by the Scottish sentries in the meadows, as he was coming up the water in a boat'[19]. Notice of this unfortunate victim's demise would suggest the continued use of small boats for re-supply.

By this time an increasingly serious threat was developing in Scotland itself as Montrose embarked upon his remarkable 'Year of Miracles'. Callendar and Lindsay were drawn off early in September, taking three cavalry and one infantry regiments north, the former officer returned though the troops would be needed to oppose Montrose and his lieutenant Alastair MacColla[20]. Nonetheless, siege operations progressed. By 7 September Leven was predicting 'a short end of the work' – as ever he was inclined to place more reliance upon his sappers than his gunners. Parliamentary sympathisers in London were equally anxious to place a positive 'spin' on the progress of the siege:

> [Leven] had with wonderful art and resolution, and success and speed, almost at once begun his galleries and completed them; and his eager soldiers invade the town with their eyes, and are by-and-by to invade it with their arms. Newcastle is also said to be very wilful, and will not listen to counsels for it sown safety …[21]

This idea that the citizens are authors of their own tribulations is a common one in Parliamentary propaganda; that they are fissiparous and misguided, that their stance is contrary to the common weal. Besides, coal had reached famine prices in the capital. Royalists far distant in Oxford observed the siege with relative disinterest and the faction within the town must have felt largely abandoned. Their stand is thus viewed as perverse by their enemies but this takes no account of the townsmen's long history of association with the Crown and the identification by the ruling elite of their obligations and close ties to Charles I.

Leven expressed this confidence in the text of a further summons; 'endeavour to acquit yourselves like rational men, which is the last advice in this kind you are like to receive from us as your friends.' To accompany these diplomatic overtures, leaflets inciting the citizens to lay down arms were chucked over the walls by the sackful. Marley returned a further courteous but stiffly defiant response; 'we fear not your threats, your cannon, nor what can be invented against us …'[22]. Brave words all round, but the plain fact was that Glemham, who might have been attempting relief from Carlisle, remained impotent and immobile, daily the vice was tightening and there was a growing body of opinion within the walls that favoured agreeing to terms. To many, persistence seemed to smack more of hubris than logic. Commerce was at a standstill, damage considerable, discomfort and privation deepening.

David Leslie, an energetic and capable cavalry officer, had forayed against the Royalists in Cumberland and Westmorland, bottling up any likely effort from that quarter. For the Royalists in Newcastle, no other viable hopes remained. Leven's response to Marley's defiance was to unleash Baillie's battery on the Leazes which, after three hours' bombardment, brought down a section of wall, 'opening a practicable breach the wall fell down within half a yard of the root, and so large that ten might have marched through it in a front.' No actual assault followed, affording the defenders an opportunity to fill the gap with improvised barricades. It is said that shot fired from the tower of St Andrew's Church fatally interrupted the flow of one of Douglas' colleagues as he preached in the open[23]! Very soon *Mercurius Aulicus* was boasting of the defenders' further sorties; 'The Scots before Newcastle are neither numerous nor courageous, being bravely tamed by that excellent blow which the garrison bestowed upon them … at which two times the brave men of Newcastle slew and took above 500 Scots …' brave deed indeed but doubtless wildly exaggerated, casualties were more likely counted in single figures.

Providence returned to favour the Newcastle men on Monday 23rd, an incident recounted in a sermon preached by George Wishart, Lecturer in St Nicholas. He recorded that on the day a new magistrate had been elected, a stray round-shot passed clear between the sword-bearer and senior justice, who had briefly halted and thus avoided dismemberment. Wishart clearly felt this was the work of 'he who directed the stone of David's sling against the brain pan of Goliath'[24]. It also appears that Callendar had been temporarily detached to provide assistance to Argyll. Montrose was already making his presence felt and the Campbell chief was under pressure. He was soon to return, however, ill-advisedly perhaps, as Montrose would go on to win yet more spectacular victories.

That Sunday, the besieged received further intimations of the Almighty's goodwill. Their sappers, engaged in counter-mining, discovered one of the Scots mines by Sandgate that sunk closest to the river. Lithgow confirms a further three shafts were already being dug and Callendar had the initial charge exploded to save the garrison from finishing the job by flooding the mine – habitual recourse in these circumstances. In his daily sermon, Wishart had yet further cause to thank providence which had apparently frustrated an attempt to ignite the garrison's own magazine 'whereby many of us had been miserably massacred, and the rest made an easy prey and spoil to our cruel enemies'[25]. Meanwhile, the Scots officers continued to grouse over the lack of supplies, both victuals and cash. Wishart, as ever, was ready with a rousing sermon to stir the defenders. Even this run of minor successes could not disguise the seriousness of Newcastle's plight:

> Let us be of good courage and play the men, and behave ourselves valiantly, and God
> will do what seemeth him best; and let no man say, 'oh, our help is far from us' … I attest
> the consciences of you all when you look back into the weeks and months of the siege

which are already passed … what thought you that this handful of ours could not only have resisted that equally mighty and malicious enemy; but also so often beaten, killed, and taken them in their very forts and works …[26]

This martial discourse, celebrating in a most un-Christian manner the taking off of so many Scots, ended with exhortations to remain obdurate and give no thought to compromise. More good news followed; in total three more mines were discovered and flooded that week. Lithgow, dour as ever, observed, 'the enemy growing insolent, gave order for ringing of bells all night.'

Final Demands

News circulating in London was still putting an altogether more favourable spin on the situation. Reports claimed the Scottish guns were wreaking havoc and causing widespread destruction, that food was running out, that an outbreak of the flux was taking numerous lives, that the forts either at North or South Shields were changing hands in fierce fighting. It was suggested that only Marley's intransigence was holding the besieged to their places and that the mayor had attempted to bribe Leven to the tune of £30,000. Much of this was mere hype yet the city was in dire straits. On 14 October Leven sent a final demand; this was somewhat less cordial in tone:

As you will be answerable to God and these whom it may concern, if in these things you fail, you may then expect the extremities of war, and we profess ourselves, and the army under our conduct to be altogether free and innocent of whatever bloodshed and other calamities may ensue through your obstinacy[27].

An equally defiant response was returned: 'We declare to you and all the world that we keep this town for the use of his majesty …' Leven, in turn, answered that he was willing to exchange hostages and parlay. Whilst Marley temporised and sent a vacillating reply he did not close the door on negotiations. More finely tuned correspondence ensued, Leven taking exception to what were obviously mere delaying tactics. Letters passed back and forth as the two sides crept towards acceptable terms for parlay. These negotiations required considerable finessing; who should be sent as hostages and who should be appointed to treat as commissioners. At length, Colonel Charles Brandling, Lieutenant Colonel Thomas Davieson and Captain Cuthbert Carr were sent from the city. Marley, Sir Nicholas Cole and Sir George Baker with a single secretary formed the negotiating team[28]. On 18 October at 9 o'clock in the morning the hostages were sent out via Sandgate and the Scots commissioners entered. Leven had appointed Sir Adam Hepburn, his treasurer, Sir David Hume and John Rutherford with their own secretary.

It is somewhat difficult to fathom the defenders' intentions at this juncture and, frustratingly, our understanding is derived from the Scottish sources, whose impartiality can scarcely be counted on. The upshot is that the talks were merely a screen for further delay on Marley's part yet we must wonder what he hoped to gain. Time was not in any way of the essence. There was no real hope of relief. Glemham was effectively corralled in the west, the King's Oxford army far too far away and there was no prospect of a relief from any other quarter.

The best that the defenders could hope was that the onset of winter might somehow force the Scots to abandon their siege. Given the vast investment of materiel and resources this appeared most unlikely. The battering of the walls by Newgate had shown how swiftly breaches could be opened and, given the very long odds, there was no real prospect of beating off a determined assault. Leven was demonstrably running short of patience. The meeting of both sets of commissioners on 18 October proved frustrating as Sir Adam Hepburn recorded:

> The Mayor, Sir Nicholas Cole and Sir George Baker, were treating with us; they gave us big words; do what we could, they would not so much as come to speak of conditions for rendering up the town; after three or four hours debate, all that we could draw from them was, that they would think upon our propositions, and return them within three or four days[29].

Preparations

When the Scots reported to their commander, he was clearly exasperated and resolved to settle the matter next day by trial of arms, in the afternoon Leven 'set to work against the town'. Callendar's batteries were deployed to bring fire upon the south eastern and south western flank of the town at Sandgate and Closegate respectively. Foot battalions moved up onto the higher ground near the stream by Barras Bridge. So thin were the ranks of the defenders that Marley ordered the evacuation of the Shieldfield fort; he needed the 300-strong garrison manning the city walls. The place was torched as the defenders withdrew. This evident preparation did, doubtless as the Scottish general had hoped, serve to concentrate the minds of the councillors, who wrote to him that evening. Their tone was distinctly more upbeat and they asked only that he hold off till Monday by when they would revert fully to him with detailed proposals.

Leven summoned an urgent council of war with his officers, no easy matter as these were widely scattered but a swift reply was drafted and sent. As ever the Scot was punctilious but spoke plainly that he would brook no more prevarication. Terms for the surrender were exact and the defenders were instructed to give note of their submission to Lord Sinclair's quarters by six o'clock next morning, their intent evidenced by the rendition of a further group of hostages 'and if you fail in sending out these hostages ... I shall take it as a refusal, and give up all treaty ...'

The terms offered were by no means unduly onerous. Officers and men who wished could march out with all arms and baggage and proceed where they chose. Any citizens who so wished could follow; sick and infirm residents would receive full care; those who stayed should have no fear of mishandling from the Scots. Those ancient rights and privileges of the city would be guaranteed; gentlemen who chose to retire to their country houses should do so freely, there would be no free quarter for Scottish troops and only a modest garrison installed. All in all, these were generous terms[30]. Promptly, at 6 o'clock the next morning, 19 October, the Scottish batteries boomed, targeting their shot at Sandgate, Pilgrim Street Gate, Westgate and below the White Friars Tower. The bombardment lasted for two hours, by which time Marley's final response reached Leven.

This was not encouraging. The mayor persisted in his earlier vacillation – he reminded Leven that it was the Scots who had demanded terms rather than the council offer them. He does not refuse the summons outright but asks for a further delay till Monday 21st for a considered response, 'the delivery of Newcastle is not of so small moment'. Marley goes on to intimate there are further articles to be negotiated prior to formal surrender. This intransigence came as no surprise, Hepburn confirms it was more or less what the Scots had been expecting, hence their show of firepower. For the covenanters further delay was unacceptable, the winter was indeed drawing on, maintaining the siege lines very costly and the defenders' counter-mining threatened to flood more of their own galleries, 'so many of our mines as they had not found out or drowned were in danger of their hourly finding out ... and our soldiers were earnest [anxious] to have some end of the business'[31]. Both sides would be affected by continuing supply difficulties, exacerbated as autumn progressed.

Leven sent no reply and Marley wrote now to Sinclair, a rather disordered communication, suggesting Leven was somehow dead and 'wishing you could think of some other course to compose the differences of these sad distracted kingdoms, than by battering Newcastle ... Leven drily confirmed he was still drawing breath and hoped he might do him [Marley] some service yet before he died.

The time for talking was now ended.

Storming the Walls – 19 October 1644

Woe to that breach beside Black Bessie's Towre,
Woe to itself that bloudy butchering bower!
Where valiant Home, that stern Bellona's blade,
And brave commander fell; for there he stay'd
Arraigned by death.

Anon.

When you determine to risk a battle, reserve to yourself every possible chance of success, more particularly if you have to deal with an adversary of superior talent, for if you are beaten, even in the midst of your magazines and your communications, woe to the vanquished.

Napoleon Bonaparte

The attacker's massed brigades drew up in a chill morning air, breath streamed in the capricious breeze, carrying intimation of winter around the corner. The dark-clad ministers ranted of God's truth. Pike and shot were in their ranks, a forest of points raised against a grey sky. Ahead, the breaches gaped like fresh wounds on the body of those ancient walls, scarred and flayed by shot. Rubble torn from the shattered stone spilled outwards like the devils' ramp, inviting, taunting, men to glory and to Hell. Behind, crouched, matches lit, the defenders waited, their throats dry.

The Ring

Even William Lithgow, not one to go overboard with admiration, had viewed Newcastle's walls as formidable, more so in his opinion 'than those of York, and not unlike to the walls of Avignon, but especially of Jerusalem.' Though the city walls were strong and the castle well sited on its prominent bluff, the defences were vulnerable to bombardment on three sides, east, west and south. The Pandon Burn, to the east, cut through a valley on its course to the Tyne. This ground rose considerably and lay a mere half mile from Sandgate. Where the ramparts strode along the western flank of Pandon Dene there was little prospect for a direct assault and, until its abandonment, had been covered by the Shieldfield Fort. Lithgow is more precise when he gives us an excellent description of the fort:

>…standing on a moderate height and champion-like commanding the fields; the model thus: it stands squarely quadrangled, with a four cornered bastion at every angle, and all of them thus quadrate, they are composed of earth and wattles; having the north-east side of one bulwark pallisaded, the rest not, save along the top of the work about, they had laid masts of ships to beat down the assailants with their tumbling force. At the entry whereof there is a wooden drawbridge, and within in two Courts 'du Guard', the graffe [ditch] is dry and of small importance, save only that repugnancy of the defendants [defenders] within, which commonly consisted of three hundred men [Brand's dimensions][1].

West of the fort stood a now-vanished windmill and, as the circuit of walls faced north, the ground offered little to excite an artilleryman. Just in front of Pilgrim Street Gate, say a quarter of a mile or so, a level swell rose with a lateral ridge running from Newgate to the Leazes. Here, on the west, the wall was more fully exposed and offered a tempting prospect. As the curtain swung towards the river, yet more high ground from Elswick and Benwell favoured an attacker. The sharp drop towards Closegate and the riverside was less attractive but the steep bank facilitated mining operations. The city was, by any standards, notwithstanding that the medieval walls were unsuited in an age of artillery, a very difficult nut to crack.

The Scottish Guns

Leven placed reliance on both mines and ordnance; he may have underrated the potency of the latter. The great guns were to punch holes in the wall at Closegate, Newgate – dubbed by Lithgow as 'Black Bessie's Tower' and by Carliol Tower[2]. Four batteries had been placed; that on the south-west probably lay on the site of the present General Hospital, affording the gunners a clear field of fire from Westgate to Closegate[3]. Baillie, whose nemesis would be the Marquis of Montrose at Kilsyth[4], had successfully breached the walls near Newgate on 7 September, firing from positions on the Leazes. Leven's north-east battery would have been placed past the stream crossed by Barras Bridge, where gunners would have a clear view of Pilgrim Street Gate and Carliol Tower at a range of about a third of a mile[5]. Sandgate boasted two gun positions, one battery being laid to cover the extensive mining being undertaken along this section. Counter-battery fire had been directed from the Shieldfield fort but the walls, particularly at Sallyport, had taken a heavy battering[6]. Callendar's additional guns on the Gateshead side could sweep the Quayside, also bringing down fire upon the castle and its outworks.

With a total train of 120 larger pieces, Leven did not lack adequate firepower, a weight of shot the defenders could never hope to match. Sandy Hamilton's newly designed and highly portable twelve-pounders certainly played their part, though it would seem that the more potent twenty-four-pounder was a favoured siege weight. Such weapons were not effective at much over 1,000 yards and most devastating at say 400. The average distance from the various locations given above is from 700–800 yards, thus within effective shooting range[7].

Throughout the continuance of the siege Marley's men had flooded or otherwise slighted more than half a dozen mines but a further quartet of devices were blown during or just prior to the main assault. Two were at Sandgate, one each at White Friar Tower and Westgate. There is some disagreement as to precisely when these were fired – Lithgow states that beneath White Friar Tower and one of the pair at Sandgate went up at 3 o'clock in the afternoon and the last two a couple of hours later. Mines, properly laid, were capable, literally, of blasting whole sections of the wall skywards, offering stunned defenders no opportunity to remedy the gaping breach – such operations are as old as war itself. Scots gunners also played their part. More sections of ancient wall were prised open at Closegate, between Andrew Tower and Newgate, between Pilgrim Street Gate and Carliol Tower and perhaps also at Sandgate[8]. In all, Scottish mines and ordnance blasted six major gaps in the defences. With the slender resources available Marley could not hope to plug even half of these sufficiently to withstand infantry assault.

For the townspeople who would, to a degree, have become accustomed to the daily routine of bombardment and counter battery work, this must have seemed like the dawn of the Apocalypse. The noise would have been terrific, like a hundred express trains charging through the streets, with buildings shaking with each reverberating blast. Houses that were struck by random shot collapsed like packs of cards, burying the inhabitants. Shards of stone and lethal wood splinters flew through the air like shrapnel. This furious tempo continued throughout the morning until the mines were sprung, adding yet fresh terror, as though the hand of God was picking up random sections of the town and scattering their fabric as dust.

The Scottish Infantry

Outside, as Scottish foot brigades formed up under arms awaiting their orders, their officers cast dice, black being the desired result, to see who should command at which points[9]. The post of maximum danger was much coveted, 'hurry to meet death lest another take your place'. Here was opportunity, probably the last as the war was seen to be winding down. If an ambitious young firebrand wanted advancement and honours these would only be found where the fight raged thickest, trusting in the invulnerability of youth.

The first of four tercios was deployed in three brigades each of two battalions, standing behind the batteries on the western flank. First into the attack here would be Loudon-Glasgow (Lord Loudoun) and Tweeddale (Scott of Buccleuch), regiments both led by their colonels, storming the breach at Closegate. Next, the Clydesdale (Sandy Hamilton, General of Artillery) and Edinburgh men (James Rae) would attempt that gap blown by the mine below White Friar Tower. Lastly, the men of Galloway (Wm. Stewart) and Perthshire (Lord Gask) would assault Westgate.

Moving north towards Newgate a second tercio waited. Baillie, as commanding officer, would lead the Angus men, the Strathearn (Lord Cowper), Fife (Lord Dunfermline), East Lothian (Sir Patrick Hepburn) and one other unmanned regiment. Baillie's tercio was the most potent, a tribute to the strength of Newgate. Opposite Pilgrim Street Gate stood the regiments of Kyle & Carrick (Lord Cassillis), Nithsdale & Annandale (Douglas of Kilhead), Mearns and Aberdeen (the Earl Marischall), Linlithgow & Tweeddale (Master of Yester), and finally the Merse Battalion (Sir David Hume of Wedderburn). Callendar had the fourth tercio in hand at Sandgate comprising Lord Sinclair's Levies, the Stirling men (Lord Livingstone), bolstered by strong companies or rather *ad hoc* units under Sir John Aytoun, Sir John Wauchope of Niddrie and the Master of Cranstoun[10]. In reserve were most probably the Midlothian, Teviotdale and Ministers' Regiments[11].

Numbers Deployed

Terry has provided a detailed analysis of the strength of the Scottish attacking force. This is based upon a total of 140 companies at an average of ninety soldiers per company, reflecting the stated strength of the foot in January 1644 as 18,000. I support Stuart Reid's more modern estimation and, allowing for casualties, sick and deserters (clearly a major problem), I would not suggest that the average company strength was greater than fifty, this provides a total of 7,000 men in the assault, rather than 12,600 which Terry suggests.

Furthermore, I would be inclined to lay some emphasis upon the matter of desertions from the Scots army. Leven complains of the high level of disaffection in his correspondence and it may have been this factor which prompted Marley to continue in his prevarication. The only hope for the Royalists within was that the Covenanters without would wither and fade away as desertion levels reached chronic proportions, finally compelling Leven to abandon the siege. My assessment of numbers has a consequentially diminishing effect on the overall distribution set out by Terry who, does allow for wastage to offer a lower total of 10,500. For the reasons given I still consider this too high.

The same reasoning must be applied to Callendar's division which had, of course, seen less campaigning and thus less loss than the rest of the army. Numerous units were stationed in outposts and Terry assesses Callendar's total strength as no more than 3,000. I see no reason to dispute this other than to observe the actual total might have been a shade less. What is clear is that his men took no direct part in the assault on 19 October, they likely formed a strategic reserve and provided infantry cover for those batteries on the Gateshead side.

Nonetheless, the defenders remained massively outnumbered, even allowing for my slashing of totals. Lithgow affirms 'they were but eight hundred of the Trained Band, and some nine hundred besides, of volunteers, pressed men [conscripts], colliers, keel-men and poor tradesmen; with some few experimented [experienced] officers to overtop [command] them'[12]. Tantalisingly few details of how these slender forces were deployed have survived. Cuthbert Carr may have commanded at Newgate. Captain George Errington, Lieutenant William Robson and Thomas Swan held Pilgrim Gate with 180 chosen men. At both points the defenders fought with great gallantry, holding on even when the defence generally had collapsed, sallying out from time to time to drive off their foes. Errington's men, who amazingly suffered no serious loss, even fired upon those of their friends who later called upon them to capitulate! We know that Sir John with a determined party of diehards fell back into the castle and its improvised outworks when all others were overrun.

Into the Breaches

Another frustrating element in the story of the siege is that most reports of the actual fighting again come from the pens of Scottish officers. Adam Hepburn provides a terse, pragmatic description such as would delight any staff-college lecturer though, from the historian's perspective, some greater subjectivity might add some insight. He reports on the deployment of the troops as described above and goes on to described how fighting, particularly around Carr's position at Newgate, became intense:

> Great dispute was made here, and some of our officers killed … They within the town made all the opposition they could, on the walls and in the streets. Some houses are burnt, the Major and some others are fled to the Castle and did presently beat a parley, which the General [Leven] would not hear, at that time, in respect they had been the instrument of so much bloodshed[13].

Lithgow provides a gritty account of the nature of the assault:

> … so also I say the breaches of the walls by batteries, being made open and passable, and ladders set to at diverse parts for scalleting [scaling], then entered mainely and manfully all the regiments of our commanded men at all quarters, but more facily [easily] and less dangerous where the mines sprung. The greatest difficulty and mightiest opposition, nay, and the sorest slaughter we received was at the climbing up of these steep and stay breaches, where truly, and too truly, the enemy did more harm with hand grenades than either with musket pike or Herculean clubs.

These clubs were anti-personnel weapons devised for just such work, like long, heavy version of a medieval spiked mace 'it grimly looked like to the pale face of murther [murder]'.

If there had perhaps been on thing the citizens would dread more than the bombardment, it would be its cessation, for that could imply only one thing, that the assault was about to commence. Then the drums would beat out the tempo, a regular cadence taken up by each boy till the noise swelled to a crescendo, banners unfurled, whipping in the autumn breeze. With nervous, clumsy fingers men bit on cartridge and blew on their match. The effective range of a musket was no more than fifty paces though sharpshooters from both sides would already be duelling. From the walls the steady columns would come in, a forest of pikes.

Leven's official dispatch, whilst commendably concise, does provide some greater measure of detail:

> The word was given and the sign made, to give fire to the rest of the mines, and for the regiments to advance all at once towards the breaches, and those places of the wall which were opened by the mine; but he met with no small opposition, and nothing was left undone by the enemy to repel the fury of the assault. They played very hotly and desperately from the castle upon the breaches, and from the flanking towers of the walls with scattered shot; yet the regiments advanced without any shrinking, though the

cannon played from many places upon their full open bodies, so that the difficult access
to the breaches and the mighty advantages of their walls and works within the town,
made a considerable loss of soldiers and officers of good quality[14].

This was the killing time. As the Scots drew near the rubble-strewn ramps, musket and
cannon would contest every step. Grimly, with levelled pikes and clubbed muskets, the
attackers pressed on. Those making the assault would be the cream of the army, men
who could be relied upon to charge home, regardless of loss. Clearly casualties were high
and desperate defenders exacted a fearful toll. As the fight came to 'push of pike', men
stumbled, scrambling to find grips on blood-slicked stones, and hacked and clawed at
each-other, consumed by the adrenalin rush 'red mist' of combat. As the Scots fought
their way into Closegate, Royalist horse mounted three desperate charges, trying to push
them back, but cavalry could not contest so narrow a space with resolute pikes and regular
volleys. From here, as the official account confirms the attackers 'marched for the relief of
the rest of the breaches, and so the soldiers gave over and forsook the walls.'

With the Scots established within the ring of defences, the walls were no longer tenable
and men fled back into the streets, apart from those bastions like Newgate and Pilgrim
Gate, which doggedly maintained their resistance. Surprisingly perhaps, the Scots did not
then have to fight for possession of a warren of streets and lanes: 'for after their entry, the
soldiers did quite vanish, sheltering themselves in houses, the inhabitants kept closed their
doors, the regiments marched through the streets without any insolence or disorder'[15].
The Scottish commander is at pains to stress that his men behaved impeccably with a
strict avoidance of pillage and offering no violence to citizens not under arms. Once
the attackers had breached the ring then bodies of infantry would be told off from the
columns to secure the enceinte from within.

Those with fight left in them or who might have had cause to fear retribution had
retreated into the castle itself:

> Lindsay, sometimes Earl of Crawford, Lord Maxwell, Doctor Wishart, a man of dangerous
> temper, who had seasoned the people both before, and at the time of the siege with
> bitter malignancy. Master Grey, and Alvay[16] and others of the perverse crew, authors of
> all the evils which might justly have fallen upon the town, so exceedingly obstinate,
> according to the rules of war, did all betake themselves to the Castle[17].

Leven was making the very clear point that, as the town had refused terms and been taken
at sword-point, the Scots were at liberty to sack the place. That they did not reflects well
upon standards of discipline. The General does allow that some 'little pillage' did occur,
mainly directed against 'some houses of the meaner sort'. Robbing the poor was clearly
less reprehensible that pilfering the rich! Leven goes on to wax lyrical over his own virtue
and moderation, nonetheless though this rather reeks of pomposity the citizens had good
cause to be grateful. Other towns had fared less well and Continental sieges conducted in
like manner frequently ended in massive bloodshed.

The anonymous correspondent who writes on 20 October[18] confirms that two
Lieutenant Colonels, Hume and Henderson together with Major Robert Hepburn were

killed with around a hundred other ranks. A further account, one of two in the British Library, states the fight lasted two hours and also makes mention of scaling ladders being employed in addition to storming the breaches. A third letter in this collection offers a fascinating anecdote: 'this morning after our batteries began to play; they jeered our men from the town, bidding them "Come on you cowardly rogues, if you dare" who before night were glad to sing another song, and crave quarter for their lives.'

One who was with the Scots outside the walls was Edward Man, a noted local Puritan who found his stance somewhat out of favour with those within. Terry makes the telling point that it is a measure of the polarisation of opinion which prevailed that religious difference counted above traditional patriotism. Man's letter praises the Scots; 'I am happy God made me a spectator to the fall of these wicked men who were born to ruin so famous a town …'[19]

Douglas' account adds little of additional interest whilst Lithgow provides his more expanded view. The Scots were resisted fiercely at every breach. By Carliol Tower Lieutenant-Colonel Henderson, Major Moffat and numerous other ranks fell. At Newgate, where the fight raged fiercely, Carr's defenders accounted for Lieutenant-Colonel Home, Major Hepburn, Captains Corbet and Home. At Westgate, Captains John and Thomas Hamilton were killed, Captain Sinclair died by Sandgate. Lithgow confirms the breaches were hotly contested, as the Scots scrambled and cursed up the desperate incline they were met, as mentioned above, by showers of 'grenadoes' (grenades). The total obliteration effected by the mines proved easier than tumbles of masonry plucked down by bombardment. Lithgow relates that Callendar did personally participate in the assault, leading his column at Sandgate and clearing the Quayside with 'flying colours and roaring drums'[20].

As he broke in, Callendar sent the Nithsdale and Annandale men to clear the eastern flank of the enceinte. Lithgow tells us that although some men, as previously reported, did simply disappear into their own or other's houses, there was a final stand by the more determined defenders driven back into the Cloth Market where, caught between twin pincers, survivors laid down their arms and begged for quarter:

> The rest of our northern and western brigades pursuing hotly these shrinking fugitives from the walls to the choking market-place; where being distressed (as it were) between Scylla and Charibdis, they presently called for quarter and laying down their arms without assurance, [unconditional surrender] some were taken, some were shaken, some stood still and some fled away to hide their bleeding bodies in some secret shelter[21].

Consolidation by the Scots was perhaps less orderly than Leven's smug dispatch asserts. Lithgow reports there was some indiscipline and looting, as the Scots abused their victory in storming the town with too much undeserved mercy, so 'as they unwisely and imprudently overreached themselves in plundering the town'[22]. It was over, bar those who had fled to the uneasy sanctuary of the castle.

Here, Marley had run up a flag of truce which the Scots ignored – the mayor had tarried too long. His next letter to Leven was penned in rather less hubristic terms. He entreated that the diehards in the castle might be afforded the same terms as were offered before and allowed free passage. Optimistically, he concludes: 'And truly my Lord, I am yet confidant to receive so much favour from you, as that you will take such care of me, as that I shall receive no wrong from the ignoble spirits of the vulgar sort; for I doubt no other …'[23]. These terms were refused. In the circumstances this can hardly have come as a surprise.

When the Scots had secured their hold they found 'such scarcity of victuals and ammunition, they considered that unless one-half of the people devoured thee other, they could not have held out ten days longer.' The Scots did, however, honour 'King David's ancient rule that they who stayed with the baggage and they that fought in the field should share in the plunder alike.' Loot was an important motivator for all armies of the period and the Scots were nothing if not well organised. Leven would have chosen to turn a blind eye to the pillaging which did occur – after all, the townspeople had refused terms and were thus not entitled to any courtesies. Lithgow certainly takes the view, albeit partisan that 'no history can parallel where less cruelty and insolence, and more mercy, were shown in any town gained by storm … since the deluge of the world.'

On Sunday 20 October, Leven and his senior officers heard a sermon preached by Douglas in St Nicholas' Church; 'He maketh wars to cease unto the end of the earth, he breaketh the bow, and cutteth the spear in sunder; he burneth the chariot in the fire …' After such rousing spiritual sustenance the General, on a more practical note, strictly forbad looting and ordered all Scottish troops to leave the streets and return to their former quarters; only a minimal garrison remained. God, it subsequently appeared, was not as wholeheartedly behind the covenanters as Douglas had opined. For the next three days autumnal gales battered victor and vanquished alike, sweeping aside the pontoon bridges and obliging the Scots to seek shelter in the ravaged town.

Before the storms had abated Sir John and the other survivors had surrendered unconditionally[24]. The mayor was placed under house arrest, a strong guard was needed not to keep him in but to keep the vengeful mob out and 'defend him from the fury of the incensed people, for he is hated and abhorred by all, and he brought many families to ruin'[25]. When taken from his home to a less congenial billet in the cells, Marley was roughly handled and, when he was committed to the custody of Sheriff Whalton, the mob was baying for his blood, 'much ado to keep him from being torn to pieces'. Sir John was gaoled within the castle he had so recently held, 'where now that presumptious governor remaineth till the hangman salute his neck with a blow of "Strafford's Courtesie"' (decapitation). In fact, Marley not only survived but contrived to escape or was allowed to slip away!

Only a single Royalist bastion now remained; the medieval castle at Tynemouth, controlling the mouth of the river. As early as 1642, the marquis had installed a labour force 300 strong to repair the walls and put the place generally in defensible array – six guns had been mounted. A Scottish force had masked the place from the outset and it was know the garrison was much afflicted by an outbreak of plague. Leven was minded to heed the Governor Sir Thomas Riddell's call for parlay and was equally liberal on the matter of terms. These were similar to what had earlier been offered; that the garrison could march out with all their equipment; none would be obliged to enter into the Covenant against his will; those who simply wished to return to their homes might do so free of fine or retribution[26]. Consequently, these generous proposals were accepted and Riddell surrendered the castle on 27 October. The Civil War in the north was now effectively at an end. It now only remained to count the cost.

Aftermath – *Fortitur Triumphans Defendit*

'Now tell us what 'twas all about' Young Peterkin, he cries;
And little Wilhemine loos up
With wonder-waiting eyes;
'Now tell us all about the war,
And what they fought each other for'

'Battle of Blenheim' Robert Southey

A fortified place can only protect the garrison and arrest the enemy for a certain time. When this time has elapsed and the defences are destroyed, the garrison should lay down its arms. All civilised nations are agreed on this point …

Napoleon Bonaparte

Newcastle, for the first time in the Civil Wars, was in the hands of Parliament. Roundhead sympathisers within, so long kept down by the Cavalier faction, would have their day:

> Hugely influential both strategically and economically the city of Newcastle additionally attained a great deal of cultural and polemic significance during the war period. Although in the main ignored as a locus for loyalism by 'Mercurius Aulicus' and Oxford based tract writers, the city was regularly lambasted by London pamphleteers as the entry point for thousands of popish sympathisers and continental troops. It was not coincidence they suggested, that Henrietta Maria had landed on Tyneside when she returned from the continent; or that the Earl of Newcastle was waging such a popular and successful series of campaigns in the north-east… For Parliament the city was a potent symbol of how Royalist intransigence directly led to social and economic deprivation Newcastle became integrated into a Parliamentarian historiography and topography that used the city as a symbol to demonstrate the consequences of needless resistance to the will and interests of the people[1].

Casualties

Lithgow states that storming Newcastle cost the Covenanters a total of 299 casualties, including thirty-eight officers. Douglas and others claim rather fewer, 100 or less.

This discrepancy may be explained as perhaps representing the number who fell in the breaches with an addition by Lithgow of those who died of wounds subsequently. This is pure speculation but it would not be unexpected that numbers of those injured in the attack might succumb in the course of following days and weeks. There seems general agreement that fatalities amongst officers were especially high and we might wonder how many of those *beaux sabreurs* who threw dice the night before fell at their posts next day.

Losses amongst the defenders are far harder to assess but the consensus appears to be that these were not notably high. It would be expected that attackers, in storming the gaps, would suffer greater loss. At least one account attests to the killing of several hundred townsmen with some 300 or 400 more imprisoned[2]. Some of the fallen, such as Sir Alexander and Joseph Davison, are commemorated in St Nicholas' Cathedral[3]. Lithgow's comments on the Scots' pillaging have already been mentioned and, whilst reprehensible, these outrages do seem to represent isolated incidents and the Scottish officers appear generally to have been able to exercise fuller control.

Coals Once More

In the capital there was heartfelt relief. On 25 October the Commons passed a resolution giving thanks:

> The Lords and Commons in parliament assembled, having received certain intelligence of God's gracious Providence, in delivering the Town of Newcastle in the Hands of our Bretheren of Scotland, come in to our assistance; do Order, that public thanks be given to God on our and their behalf, by all the ministers within the cities of London and Westminster, and the lines of communication on the Lord's Day next, for this great blessing from the Lord of Hosts; and the Lord Mayor of London is desired to take care, that timely notice be given to the several ministers of the several parishes and places aforesaid[4].

Newcastle's fall naturally released the coal supply and, to all intents and purposes signalled an end to the war in the north. The Scots intervention, as hoped, had destroyed the King's hegemony, seen his northern army crushed and the Marquis of Newcastle, who had begun the year as virtual master of the region, now an exile. Londoners would not freeze that winter, 'though our London wood merchants perhaps grow chill upon the business …'

Having proved so potent a thorn in Parliament's flesh, Marley and other diehards could expect little clemency and none was offered. On 19 November some 28 of the captives were ordered to be transferred to the capital. Sir John was to be tried; others were imprisoned or barred from civic office[5]. Aside from the personal consequences to the losers, the net effect, as Terry points out, was to transfer control of the city to the anti-Royalist faction, hitherto left largely in the wilderness[6]. On 5 December the Commons appointed a local panel to take control and enforce sanctions on the defeated, though many of those affected avoided the more draconian responses which might have been anticipated[7]. Aside from Marley himself, Sir Nicholas Cole, Sir Thomas Liddell, Sir Thomas

Riddell, Sir Alexander Davison, Sir Francis Bowes, Cuthbert Carr, Ralph Cole, Ralph Cock and Dr Wishart all feature; those who John Fenwick had labelled as 'Newcastle's new-dubbed knights'. The Puritan faction led by men such as Fenwick, with likes of Bonners and Dawsons, came into their own.

Newcastle was ready for the siege and had been fully provisioned during that summer in anticipation. Of course, in a period when seasonality was given, there would have been a need to re-provision anyway by October when harvests had been brought in and animals, fattened over the summer, were to be slaughtered. Besieged as she was, Newcastle was unable to take advantage of those new supplies. Callendar's guns on the other side of the river could effectively rake the quayside, making it difficult for any large vessel to risk the passage (supposing they had managed to make it that far up river). That the fire from his Gateshead batteries proved very galling to the besieged is confirmed by Whitelock's statement that 'most of the inhabitants of the lower town fled to the high town for shelter'.

Newcastle had traditionally imported much of her food. Wheat from Kings Lynn had gone into the production of that food staple for rich and poor: bread. Wheaten bread was still very much the prerogative of the better off, barley and other grains would go into that of the lower classes making for a heavier (and possibly healthier) loaf. Inhabitants of the upland dales of Northumberland had been used to adding pea flour to the mix, a habit continued as people moved to the city. These heavier loaves had an additional advantage; they stayed fresh for longer. A big, barley loaf could last for up to three weeks in winter.

Fish, in particular, the salted variety, was an essential part of the food supply for the poor, herring brought in by the barrel or fresh fish salted locally. Newcastle Salmon refers not just to a product exported from the city but also to a spicy brine used to preserve it. Fresh fish brought in locally would complete the menu, together with vegetables and cheese. Northumbrians still used ewes' milk, something eschewed in the south, to produce a tangy and relatively inexpensive commodity traded with the city for grain. Small quantities of meat would be stretched out by stewing.

For those at the upper end of the scale, new supplies of dried fruits and sweeteners such as sugar and spices made their diet more interesting. All classes had taken to a new trend for puddings established when the notion of using pudding cloth rather than animal gut to contain food took hold. These puddings, sweet and savoury, were filling and had the great advantage that they could be produced in one pot with a soup or stew: taking on flavour and saving on that most precious commodity; fuel. For the poor, puddings were mostly grain and suet with a little flavouring if available. For the wealthier classes, the addition of spices and sugar made for variety as well as taste. Preserved meat (smoked as in bacon or ground like sausage) could be eked out with suet padding or the dense water pastry of the period and it was not unusual to find fish taking the place of meat when necessity compelled.

Revictualling the city probably implied that supplies of preserved food had been topped up. What would be harder to ensure was a supply of vegetables and fruit, which were a mainstay of the poor. Scurvy, already common, would become rife. However, it is clear from the town accounts that supplies were getting through and we have some indication of the method. There is a payment recorded in October 1644, 'match powder and shot from nine craft to the Council House and from thence to the fort'[8]. This suggests the use of small boats to offload goods coming from downriver and, presumably, then brought into the port under cover of darkness. Sadly and tantalisingly, these accounts are incomplete – we have almost no entries for July to September 1644.

Regardless of records, small craft could not keep the city fully supplied. Numbers of large ships calling at the city ran from 60 to 100 per month in more normal times. Even allowing for a substantial proportion carrying goods other than foodstuffs, this still suggests a substantial shortfall in provisions during the continuation of the siege. The economy of Newcastle had not fully recovered from the Scots of incursion of 1640 and was undoubtedly badly affected by the events of 1644. The sum total of receipts from 1 October 1643 to the last September 1644 were in the amount of £243 11s 4d[9]. Some indication of the impact of the blockade and the siege can be arrived at by considering total receipts from ballast and shipping for just one month in 1642 - £75 12s 9½d in January of that year. Those same accounts note, 'so it appears to be more paid than received this year'[10]. There then follows a list of monies lent to the Crown, broken down according to the individual loans making up a 'donation' of £2,950. Further, there is a list of uncollected rents paid in lieu to the King as loans.

Resources were available for certain forms of expenditure. Local farriers appear to have been kept busy; the bulk of expenditure for October 1644 was disbursed to meet bills for their services. Indeed, the outstanding dues for October 1642–March 1643 were paid at this time. The city also found sufficient funds to pay for additional security measures at civic buildings. There is an entry which mentions the fitting of a new band and nails to the door of the Council House and money is spent on tar barrels, straw and nails. What does disappear are entries, such as that for May 1644, when we learn the city 'Paid the poor in the Almshouse in Pudding Chare'. The 'poore in ordinary' receive no disbursements and it is fair to assume that they will have suffered disproportionately from shortages.

Lithgow reports the piteous condition of the people of Newcastle in the wake of the siege. Pickings were poor:

> The common souldiers, being only able to plunder the common people (although they might have justly stretched their hands further) had for the greatest part of them but small benefite, excepting only household stuff, as bed-cloaths, linnings, Tanned leather, calve skins, men and womens apparel, pans, pots, and plates, and such like common things[11].

Lithgow may have had his own, propagandist reasons for wishing to portray the condition of survivors as pitiable, the consequence of an ungodly polity, but we have other evidence to suggest great distress. Bourne tells us:

> A pestilence at this time raged in Sandgate, Gateshead, Tynemouth, Sunderland, and many villages near Newcastle. This, with a scarcity of provisions, and the approach of winter, induced the Scottish army to spread over the neighbouring country, leaving a strong garrison in Newcastle[12].

If conditions in the town were harsh, those outside the walls were probably worse. The region between the Tyne and the Tees was not, on the whole, a corn producing area and had traditionally relied on imports of grain through Newcastle which meant that those people most likely to be suffering severe shortages were those outside the city, who relied on it for corn supplies, exacerbated by the depredations of the Scots whose foraging parties had cleared the area of useful supplies. The inhabitants of the north must have been highly relieved that the siege did not drag on through the winter. We know that the Scottish army had great difficulty supplying themselves (even with the sequestered produce and other goods) to the extent that they had to bring in provisions from their own country.

Contemporary correspondence from Newcastle Trinity House refers to the disastrous effect the siege had had upon business. Coal and shipping had ground to a standstill, normal commercial life had been effectively suspended altogether: '... there hath been ... a long discontinuance of trading by sea; which has much disabled us in what our Corporation should have done, both concerning rent payments, the maintenance of our poor and paying of other necessary charges and offices belonging to the Corporation'[13]. We have no contemporary record of how the survivors in the shattered city reacted. Here was a thriving port and commercial centre, caught in the murderous vortex of internecine war. Most citizens would have had no experience of conflict and its attendant horrors, the action earlier in the year had left the place relatively unscathed though Marley's ruthless slighting of the suburbs would have caused much distress.

We do have records from modern sieges such as Sarajevo during the Bosnian War of the 1990s, which show the trauma of helpless civilians experience caught up in the fury and randomness of war. All normal life is suspended, few can effectively work at their trades, income dwindles, hunger bites and the day-to-day grinding discomfort and danger continue relentlessly. Bombardment reduces streets and public buildings to ruined shells. In dense packed timber-framed houses, the risk of fire is constant, the threat to life unending. At the end of it all, the nightmare of an escalade – everyone knew what had been happening in Germany where slaughter and rapine followed a storming sure as day follows night. These Covenanters had killed women and children in the wars thus far in Scotland and Ireland. In the immediate aftermath many citizens would be listless and distraught, even the conclusion of hostilities left much in the air. No citizen of any city would relish having bands of armed soldiery on the streets and though contained, there was clearly some pillage. That the people should vent their fury upon Marley is hardly surprising, after all, his dogged refusal to agree terms had conjured the whirlwind and his defiance seemingly driven by mere hubris rather than any tactical consideration.

Quite how many houses were damaged or destroyed we cannot, with any accuracy, guess at. We do know that most public buildings had suffered. St Andrew's, heavily exposed, had taken many hits. The place was roofless, its tower shattered. There is a suggestion that Marley had placed guns in the tower and restoration would take many years[14]. St Nicholas' too had received attention from the Scottish gunners. A tale that the mayor had crammed its steeple with Scottish POWs to prevent Leven from carrying out his threat to demolish the tower as a punishment for the citizens' continued defiance is probably apocryphal. All Saints', covered by the Scottish guns from Sandgate, was likewise badly battered, there was a deal of refurbishment work carried out in 1651–2[15]. True to their Calvinist colours, the Scots wilfully defaced certain monuments, iconoclasm by intent. A large panel over George Carr's monument in St Nicholas' showing Christ crucified was ruined. There is also evidence that parish churches outside the city walls suffered vandalism during the occupation[16].

As for the ancient walls and castle, these had suffered prodigiously. Mines had inflicted even greater damage than the guns. That blown at White Friar Tower had knocked down 56 or 57 yards of masonry and one exploded near Pink Tower destroyed a section of the enceinte 55 yards in length, 3 yards deep and 6 in height. Several ordinances exist from years following providing for repairs[17]. The Tyne Bridge was in need of restoration, whole districts of suburbs had been demolished by the defenders. Marley's house was one of those targeted for arson; the vicarage had already sustained significant damage. These losses fell upon a community impoverished by the siege, at its least resilient and economically inactive. Furthermore, the inhabitants were to entertain their Scottish captors until February 1647 and, whilst discipline was generally exemplary, abuses and some pilferage must have occurred. Before the city fell, Parliament had been preparing the ground for its place-men. Some ten days before the storming, Sir John and William Fenwick, Sir John and Ralph Delaval, Sir William Selby, Sir Thomas Widdrington, Sir Robert Jackson, Michael Welden and Sir Arthur Haselrig had been confirmed as Deputy-County Lieutenants for Northumberland.

The Puritan Supremacy

All was not entirely amicable between the victors. The Scots were acting as servants of the Scottish Committee of Estates and through them as agents of the Committee of Both Houses, a potentially tricky relationship. The English, on 25 October, wrote to remind their allies that the ongoing civil administration of the city, once taken, was to be entrusted to those appointed by Parliament. The Scots replied cannily that matters were perhaps not quite so clear cut. The Committee of Scotland desired that their allies should nominate a governor and provide a garrison whereupon they, the Scots, 'would endeavour to answer the expectations of both houses with all brotherly love and respect.' For the English Parliament, this was a matter of urgency; coal must again begin moving before winter exerted a grip on London. Local commissioners in the north added an urgent plea that Parliament might direct attention to the region where the upheaval of war had left so many scars; a perceived need for spiritual sustenance was also expressed: 'We daily expect some good ministers be sent into these parts, of which there is a very great want'[18]. Despite this entreaty, it was not until 5 December that Dr Jenison was appointed to replace the Royalist Alvey. Henry Warmouth was to occupy Marley's post as mayor, Edward Wright a lawyer of Gray's Inn became recorder and Robert Ellison, sheriff.

Though the civil administration of Newcastle was now very much in the hands of politically acceptable local candidates, the Scots remained in charge of military matters. It was not until 10 April the following year that Parliament appointed Sir James Lumsden as an official military governor, a post he was to hold till the Scots finally withdrew in February 1647. The Puritan supremacy was now a fact and numerous post-holders were purged to make way for more like-minded incumbents – the curates of St Nicholas' and

St Andrew's along with the headmaster of the Grammar School were removed. These Puritans lorded their success in an ordinance of 9 April 1645: 'Papists and their families' were to be ejected; here the order was clearly repeating previous bans 'notwithstanding the most of them have disobeyed the said order'[19]. Now, prompt and determined action was to be taken to ensure those adhering to the old faith and most likely high church Anglicans were driven out.

All this would be pleasing to the Scots. Both they and Parliament were acutely aware of the importance of the coal trade, not just in terms of energy supplies to the capital but as an instrument of political control. Provided all remained amicable between English Parliamentarians and their Scottish allies then the smooth flow of coals could be assured. Should the two sides disagree then the Scots could use the industry and the control it gave them as a very strong bargaining chip. The Covenanters were also proposing to levy a tax on the proceeds of the trade to pay their occupation expenses. Sir Lionel Maddison, who'd accompanied the Covenanter army, estimated the annual volume of coal from Newcastle at 180,000 chaldrons[20], along with 40,000 chaldrons from Sunderland[21]. On 13 November 1644 Parliament had reversed the earlier ordinance of January 1643 which had prohibited the trade. The revival was immediate as the groaning staithes began to clear.

On 17 November both the English and Scottish Parliamentarians agreed that the interests of Marley, Sir Thomas Riddell, Sir Thomas Liddell, Sir Alexander Davison, Sir John Minns and Sir Francis Anderson were all forfeit to the Crown. Those less tainted by overtly Royalist sentiment were left 'as tenants and servants to the Parliament' whereby they received 10s for each chaldron shipped from a fixed price of 15s, the balance being applied to meet the costs of military and naval commitments. Despite these measures, the ravaged land laboured under the burdens imposed by war and occupation, Maddison was driven to write plaintively on 27 November:

> No money is to be had, little provision left, nothing but money will give content; driving off what is remaining where money cannot be had is not only in part executed by the officers and soldiers, but generally threatened, and what the consequences thereof will be any man may judge … many are ready to run away and leave all[22].

Aftermath

As winter drew on, the Scots army settled into seasonal quarters scattered throughout the region whilst Leven returned to Scotland, his mission complete. Newcastle upon Tyne had paid a very heavy price for its allegiance to Charles I and would have to wait for the Restoration for recognition. Though the war in the north might have ended, fighting still raged throughout the three Kingdoms. Montrose was embarking upon his 'Year of Miracles', which would hold out a bright beacon of hope for Charles in 1645 as his own fortunes dipped and crashed with the loss of his veteran Oxford army at Naseby. The dashing marquis came to grief at Philliphaugh by Selkirk but the war spluttered and flared for another year until the King conceded defeat. The First Civil War was followed by the second and in Scotland the Engagers gained control only to be massively defeated by Cromwell at Preston. When the regicides demanded and got the head of Charles I this was a step too far, even for those who had so ardently championed the Covenant, and Scots armies mustered to fight for Charles II. They marched to bloody defeats at Dunbar and in the streets of Worcester. After a bitter campaign Cromwell conquered opposition in Scotland and the Committee was largely captured at Alyth. It was now Scotland's turn to feel the burden of occupation.

Fresh alarums occurred in 1648 during the Second Civil War – on 11 August Henry Lilburn, then holding the rank of lieutenant colonel, declared for the King at Tynemouth. Sir Arthur Haselrig, he of the Lobsters[23] then governor of Newcastle, responded immediately, deploying a full foot brigade and 100 dragoons to recover the place[24]. Lilburn's slender garrison was overwhelmed; he fell in the fight and his severed head was carried back on a pole!

Despite the ravages, Newcastle does seem to have recovered fairly rapidly. The restoration of the coal trade was clearly a major factor. Between 1655 and 1658, a new Guildhall and Exchange was constructed on the Sandhill at a cost of £10,000, a very sizeable budget[25].

One legacy of the siege is said to have been the city's motto, conferred after the Restoration – *Fortitur Defendit Triumphans* (Triumph by Brave Defeat). In the circumstances, this was surely well deserved! It is difficult to determine the legacy of the siege if indeed any can be discerned. The winter of 1644/5 was clearly a hard one, the citizens were defeated and occupied, morale generally, apart from amongst the Puritan clique, to whom the tragedy had proved such a Godsend, must have sunk very low. People were hungry and dispirited, even if loss of life had not been severe, everyone would know at least one or more families affected. By now the country generally was weary of war, in some districts local militias or 'Clubmen' formed simply to resist any army which marched through, regardless of faction.

As far as can be discerned, the siege left little by way of enduring folk memory or heritage. Indeed it has largely been forgotten. Professor Terry submitted his detailed papers to the Society of Antiquaries at the close of the nineteenth century since when little interest has been show. Most Civil War histories barely mention the siege, the implication being that war in the north ended with the Royalist disaster at Marston Moor and the fall of York. However, the Great Siege of Newcastle in autumn 1644 was a significant episode, not just in the history of Tyneside and the north-east but of England during what was, arguably, the most crucial period in her constitutional development.

And now, the strife over, old rivalries are forgotten; the descendant of the scot and the Whitecoat live peacefully side by side. In fifty years from this time of fighting England and Scotland, each agreeing to give up its separate parliament and government, joined the two into one great whole. The healing influence of this "Union" could not be better illustrated than by pointing to the two chief dignitaries of Newcastle today★. The Mayor, a descendant of the brave, unflinching Whitecoat; the Sheriff, a descendant of the scrupulous, adventurous Scot; the only rivalry between them now being the nobler rivalry of which can do the utmost to promote the honour and advancement of the city, once "the old walled town" of which they both are proud[26].

★This is for 1889 when Alderman Thomas Richardson was mayor and Councillor William Sutton, sheriff.

Appendix 1

The Art of War in the Seventeenth Century

The First Civil War took Britain almost by surprise – these islands had thus far been spared the carnage of the Thirty Years' War which so ravaged Germany. Nonetheless, as previously mentioned, many Scots had fought as mercenaries and learned their trade under such Continental masters as Gustavus Adolphus. By the middle of the seventeenth century the use of the musket was growing in importance, though these heavy matchlock weapons were cumbersome to carry, slow to fire and at best unreliable. Few could manage more than one round per minute. Some units, particularly dragoons, were equipped with the more manageable doglock[1], precursor to the venerable flintlock that was to dominate battlefields for so long.

Arms and Drill

The file of musketeers or 'shot' was drawn up in a body five or six ranks deep and fired by 'extraduction', each rank retiring to the rear to reload after discharging a volley or 'giving fire'. This process should, in theory, produce an almost continual roll of gunfire and the manuals of the day showed an almost balletic sense of movement, extremely hard to practise in the field with raw troops. On average, most foot regiments were still made up of about 40 per cent of pikemen – stout lads with morion helmets, breast and back with steel guards, or tassets, for the thighs. The puissant pike could range in length from 12 to 15ft, its head protected by steel bars or languets which stretched down the ash shaft. The principal function of the pike was to protect the shot from cavalry and opposing formations frequently came to 'push of pike', in some ways a kind of particularly vicious scrum with much heaving and relatively few casualties.

Pikemen usually carried short swords or hangers in addition to their body armour. The shot, on the other hand, went unarmoured, being sufficiently encumbered by the weight of the weapon itself and the forked rest used to steady the long barrel. Twelve 'apostles' hung from a bandolier[2], a flask of fine grain powder being carried for priming the piece. To load, a measure of powder was poured down the pan followed by a ball, an experienced man having three or four ready in his mouth. The charge was wadded and rammed and the piece primed. The firing mechanism or cock was operated by pressure on the trigger, which lowered the lighted match over the pan. The maximum range was generally little more than 60 yards, and wind and rain frequently frustrated the musketeers' efforts.

Ranking officers were distinguished by the use of armoured neckpieces or gorgets and carried rapiers and pole-arms such as the partizan. Sergeants carried halberds. Dragoons were essentially mounted infantry whose role encompassed scouting and guard duties, providing harassing fire against cavalry and skirmishing. Cavalry regiments were generally considered, or at least considered themselves, an élite. On the Royalist side most troopers were gentlemen or sons of gentlemen, schooled on the hunting field and with the means to mount and equip themselves. The Swede Gustavus had done away with that stately but largely ineffective manoeuvre known as the caracole and reintroduced the idea of shock tactics, troopers thundering into a charge and riding knee to knee, wheel-lock pistols discharging and not infrequently used as missiles[3], broadswords flashing.

Full armour was largely obsolescent and the traditional breast and back went out of fashion as the war progressed, displaced by the ubiquitous buff coat, the bridle arm perhaps protected by a steel gauntlet. The wheel-lock was a far more sophisticated mechanism than match, though vastly more expensive, and thus became a gentleman's weapon. The cavalry man would carry a brace of pistols holstered either side of the saddle. The mechanism comprised a serrated steel wheel which sparked when struck by a piece of pyrites held in the cock. The wheel itself was wound up like clockwork using a key. Pressure on the trigger released the spring, showering sparks into the touch-hole. Most troopers carried swords – graceful, swept and cup-hilted rapiers, or the purposeful 'Walloon' hanger[4].

Strategy and Tactics

At the time of the Civil Wars there was a debate amongst professional soldiers as to whether the Dutch or more complex but flexible Swedish system devised by Gustavus was best. Armies were mainly comprised of untrained civilians, unsuited to detailed manoeuvres. Units would very easily succumb to the terror of panic and dissolve in rout if officers failed to restrain them. Morale was, however, often higher than might be expected. Some units, most notably Newcastle's Whitecoats at Marston Moor fought virtually to the last man – such sacrifice was, however, rare. Strategic aims were often somewhat confused and conflated with local objectives. Initially, the war was largely one of regions. Newcastle's objectives in 1642–3 were to secure the north for the King, deny resources to Parliament and maintain supply routes from the Continent. In this he was successful. Overall, Parliamentarians sought to defeat the King in the field and thus oblige him to negotiate, whilst Royalists sought through victories in the field to bring Parliament to its knees.

As a consequence of what was, in effect, a failure of nerve the King, by turning aside from London after Edgehill, threw away all prospect of victory[5]. The Scots intervention in January 1644 significantly altered the strategic balance in the north, eroding Newcastle's virtual hegemony at a stroke and forcing him onto the defensive. The Siege of Newcastle that autumn was, from the defenders' viewpoint, a battle largely without strategic purpose. Parliament needed to restore coal supplies to the capital. Without hope of relief, Marley could scarcely justify defiance yet, by obliging the Scots to sit down before the walls, these troops were prevented from taking the offensive against the King and were obliged to eat up a deal of treasure for no gain. By holding out Marley denied the succour of coal supply to the enemy. That said, resistance was, from the outset, largely futile and could only delay the inevitable whilst not affecting the outcome.

A typical regiment of foot was divided into ten companies, each of 100 men save the colonel's company which was at double strength. These companies were commanded by field officers and the rest by captains; a ratio of two-thirds shot to one-third pike was the norm. In battle the regiment deployed the pikes in the centre with the shot drawn up on the flanks. A field army would form up in three or four lines with the foot in the centre and the horse commanding the flanks, dragoons being used as skirmishers. Behind this screen the first line would move forward and deliver a series of volleys before both sides came to 'push of pike'. If assailed by horse, the pikes would form a defensive hedge sheltering the shot[6].

The regiment was also the typical tactical unit for cavalry, though no set standards existed. The horse might be divided into six troops, commanded by field officers and the rest by captains. A fighting formation of three ranks was usual, though for full shock effect the horse would advance six ranks deep[7]. Medical care was rudimentary, regimental surgeons existed but many wounded succumbed to shock, loss of blood or disease. Contemporary accounts stress the horrors of the battlefield with heaps of dead and wounded left unattended, exposed to the savage mercies of climate and scavengers. The fallen were ruthlessly stripped of all they possessed and local people were often less than sympathetic to men who had hitherto looted and pillaged at will.

Appendix 2

Siege Warfare

The science of artillery was growing in scope and importance; lighter field-pieces were stationed on the flanks of foot battalions and heavier pieces were sited to fire over the heads of the soldiery. Redoubts, sconces and bastions were thrown up to accommodate the heavy guns and the Swedish practice of assigning two light-field guns to each foot regiment was almost universally adopted. Round-shot was the customary missile, supplemented by case shot (a canister of musket balls which could scythe down whole files at close range). Each piece was serviced by a gunner, his mate and one or more labourers or matrosses. An army was commanded by a captain-general, assisted by a staff and a lieutenant-general or field-marshal. The foot were similarly commanded, a general, his lieutenant, and a major-general, customarily a professional soldier, often a rarity in Civil War armies. Command of the horse was similarly structured and the general of ordnance commanded the artillery.

It is probably fair to assert nonetheless, that field artillery at this date was less effective than heavy siege guns which could mercilessly flay and demolish walls designed before the age of gunpowder. If the diminutive robinet threw a ¼lb shot, the grand cannon-royal at the other end of the spectrum fired a 60lb ball. Projectiles were generally iron, though stone was not unknown, case shot could be used at close quarters to deadly effect. Rates of fire varied according to conditions and the gunner's skill, ten rounds per hour for a demi-cannon would be very respectable – the heavier the gun, the slower the rate of fire. To service a heavier piece would require a crew of say three gunners and twice as many matrosses. Gunners often christened their pieces with nicknames – 'Roaring Meg', The Queen's Pocket Pistol', 'Sweet Lips' and 'Kill-Cow'[1].

Potentially lethal and highly effective in siege operations was the stubby-barrelled mortar which threw an explosive shell over a high, arcing trajectory to fall within the defended area. These plunging missiles could destroy building and start fires, their psychological effect was considerable, no garrison could sleep safely or take its ease away from the walls[2]. To demolish barricades or stout gates the besieger might instruct a petardier. This was a somewhat risky trade for the bell-shaped charge had to be affixed to the object before being exploded. The petardier was exposed both to the hostile intent of the defenders and to the inherent risk of being caught in the blast from his device thus 'hoist with his own petard'. It is suggested that petardiers required the solace of strong liquor before proceeding. In the circumstances this is entirely understandable.

Engineers were usually skilled professionals recruited for their specialism. Most of the labouring was undertaken by pioneers who were less elevated, often troops that were below front line status or had failed in their baptism of fire. In a siege situation citizens would be conscripted, male and female alike, to dig trenches and throw up earth works[3]. As the outbreak of war caught the nation unawares and after a long interval of peace, most castles and towns were only posessed of their ancient medieval fortifications, rendered redundant by gunpowder. The only recourse for a defender therefore was the vast effusion of sweat, backed by ingenuity and professional guidance to throw a circle of redoubts around these old walls to create an outer ring of earth and timber fortifications capable of resisting shot. For the attacker, once he had assessed the strength of the defender's lines he would dig a series of trenches, or parallels, out of range of the enemy guns, then creep these forward with zigzag lines or saps until he dug an inner line within which to site his own guns. Once the artillery had effected a breach or series of breaches, the assault could be delivered. The honour of leading the storming party – later called 'Forlorn Hope' (from the German Verlorner Hauf – 'lost party') was hotly contested amongst junior officers. Risky as this was, success was a sure path to advancement.

Siege warfare was far from glamorous. It was dangerous for both besieger and besieged, dirty and pestilential, with long periods of tedious discomfort enlivened by moments of murderous intensity. Snipers would be active from both sides and conditions within the enceinte would quickly become foul, whilst the besiegers would fare little better. Once a breach was effected those within would attempt to limit the damage by sealing off the rupture, studding the rubble with *cheavaux de frise* (spike studded obstacles) and throwing up an inner barricade behind. Once an attacker was obliged to attempt an escalade the niceties of war were undone, the besieged could expect no terms from that point[4]. Most traces of Civil War sieges have now vanished, but the battlefield detective may find some reward in perseverance[5]. Gabions provided a moveable and efficient protection for the gunners and matrosses, with timber decking to facilitate and soak up the massive recoil from the great guns. The crack and bellow of these devil's toys was truly terrifying. Modern film depictions are somewhat lacklustre by comparison, nor do the ever show the savage kick as the gun leaps backwards on discharge, any unwary soul in the path of several tons of timber and iron would be crushed outright or maimed.

It was the experience of war in the Low Countries[6] which showed the effectiveness of more *ad hoc* fortification comprising mainly turf and timber; the flexibility of these materials provided excellent protection. Parliament's stout defence of Lyme relied entirely upon substantive earthworks with blockhouse walls some 12ft thick[7]. If there was insufficient time and/or labour to construct these gargantuan outer rings then the best defenders might do was to pile earth behind old masonry walls to add an extra cushion against shot. For the besieger or would-be besieger a properly dug and prepared series of defences, adequately manned and with sufficient weight of shot on the ramparts, presented a fearsome obstacle. First steps for the attacker were to try and isolate the stronghold and create a ring around the ring – lines of circumvallation. This was an ancient art. One of the most famous classical sieges, that of Alesia in Gaul by Caesar in 52 BC, required the Romans to completely seal off the massive hilltop oppidum by extended lines of circumvallation and thereafter to construct an outer shell – or lines of contravallation around their own works to protect the besiegers from relieving forces; a truly Olympian undertaking. True to the old maxim of sweat saves blood, Caesar's great victory at Alesia proved the worth of absolute thoroughness.

During the era of the Civil Wars, the besiegers' works could assume vast and elaborate proportions, beginning with the initial ditch excavated so the earth or spoil was flung inwards to form the basis of a palisade. Thereafter, to protect their troops against sallies by the defenders[8], the attackers would stud their works with bastions, redans, redoubts, additional breastworks and even sconces. As might be imagined, these lines, like Caesar's, could extend over a considerable distance, in the case of Newark this was something over 14 miles[9]. Once the besiegers were secure in their lines and their batteries in position, it was time to creep forward a series of strongpoints into no-man's-land. From these, encroaching trenches snaked towards the walls, so dug as to minimise any risk of defilade. This was hazardous work, the leading sapper was protected by a gabion which, laid flat, was rolled before him as he struggled to make the first cut, followed by comrades who continued the work of excavation. These gabions would be used to line the parapet. Commanded parties of shot would provide covering fire whilst the besiegers' guns sought to flay the ramparts with suppressing fire. If the ground was hard or stony then trenches would have to be made up from spoil, gabions and blindes. Assuming the attackers managed to work their trenches sufficiently close to the defences then this might be a signal for parlay, the garrison might be sufficiently demoralised to consider terms, knowing that the span for these must end once this delicate point in the leaguer was past.

It was by no means necessary for a garrison to hide behind their ramparts awaiting the inevitable. Defenders could, and frequently did, mount raids or sallies from the walls, to destroy the attacker's works, spike his guns, interdict his supplies and beat up his quarters generally. Indeed, this level of energy was expected from a competent commander.

> Sir Thomas Venn advised: … the first beginning is to keep the enemy from the town as far off and as long as you can. Therefore whatsoever without the works can put a stop to the enemy, the besieger [in this context the besieged] must possess and defend as long as they can. They must use all their endeavour to hinder the approach of the enemy, therefore let them sally frequently, but warily lest they fall into snares to the irreparable loss of the town[10].

No fortress or town, however resolute the defenders, could hope to hold out indefinitely. At some point the besiegers' fire – relentless, skilled battering from the great guns would open breaches. For defenders this implied the full horrors of storm and sack, their only hope at this point being the possibility of relief, unless they could effectively seal off the breaches and met the attackers at push of pike, driving them off.

The Artillery Train or 'Trayne'[11] might be made up as follows:

General of the Artillery
Lieutenant General
Comptroller (Chief of Staff)
Commissary (logistics)

10 Gentlemen of the Ordnance (officers)

25 Conductors (NCOs)

2 Comptrollers of Fortifications

1 Master Gunner

136 Gunners

1 Master Fireworker (explosives)

2 Battery Masters

1 Master Carpenter

12 Carpenters

1 Petardier

2 Waggon Makers

2 Gabion Makers

2 Harness makers

1 Cooper

2 Farriers

1 Surgeon

1 Surgeon's Mate

1 Captain of Miners

25 Miners

25 Pioneers (labourers)

1 Trench Master

1 Waggon master

Appendix 3

The Scots Army

There are a number of excellent books on Covenanting armies, including Professor Terry's definitive two-volume history. An excellent introduction is to be found in *Stuart Reid's Scots Armies of the 17th Century (1) The Army of the Covenant 1639–1651* (Partizan Press; Leigh-on-Sea). Clearly it is not possible here, nor necessary to provide a definitive description. What follows is merely a series of notes to assist the reader in understanding the nature of the forces deployed during the Siege. It should be stressed that the army of the Covenant was a Scottish National Army, a regular force raised and recruited by the government of the northern kingdom. That there was a Royalist faction from 1644, in the form of Montrose and Alasdair MacColla, need not overly concern us. The Scottish polity was not therefore split as was the case in England. The army which crossed the Tweed in 1640 and again in 1644 was not a faction, but the military might of the realm; a united, professionally lead, army.

Certainly during the brief fury of the Second Bishops' War the Scots were infinitely better prepared than the English forces seeking to oppose them. It cannot be overstated that this was very much a national army almost in the modern sense. It fought for the lawful government and was, in these early days, not riven by factions, united in faith, well disciplined and well officered – a formidable instrument of war. In practice, one might suspect the majority of both officers and enlisted men were probably both apolitical and neutral in their religious persuasion. Traditionally, the Scots tended toward light-fingeredness, and looting was not necessarily frowned upon. Excesses were rare and likely to be perpetrated against their own countrymen. Montrose's female camp followers were cut up whilst foraging before Kilsyth and women and children who trailed in the wake of his defeated force at Philiphaugh were brutally done to death under the rabidly enthusiastic guidance of the Kirk.

Whilst the Scottish system allowed scope for volunteers, the principal mode of recruitment was by conscription. Committees of War, not unlike Commissions of Array were established in each district with an agreed quota[1]. In the early days of the Civil War this process worked well; it was not until the latter years when energies and resources waned that difficulties arose. The wild rush which arose before the First Bishops' War when the Scottish faith system appeared under threat was less evident four years later[2]. By the end of July 1643 the Estates had instructed the recruitment of five foot companies and three of horse, these to be mustered by mid-September[3]. In August the sum of

£40,000 Scots was set aside to pay for the army's equipment, additional arms and field gear[4]. On 18 August a general mobilisation was ordered of gentry, freeholders and the citizens of Royal Burghs with each man to provide for himself according to his station. Where there was a shortfall in arms and accoutrement then it was the responsibility of landlord or feudal superior to remedy this deficiency.

This initial preparation was directed by the magnates and gentry, duly established local committees came later and prepared lists of those 'fencible'[5] men liable for service. Once the pool of available recruits was determined, the Estates could then proceed to decide upon a quota of horse and foot regiments from each of the shires. It was the Estates who issued commissions to senior officers. Regiments were thus raised on a local or regional basis though, according to custom, most were named after their colonels – one exception was the Ministers' Regiment, raised by the particular exertions of a zealous clergy and doubtless comprised of singularly devout and god-fearing recruits[6]! By the final days of December 1643, a most impressive array was mustered north of Berwick-upon-Tweed; twenty-one foot battalions, nine cavalry regiments and one of dragoons, with a nominal strength of as many as 26,000 men in all[7].

These Scots were very much warriors for the working day. Their uniform, horse and foot, was dull and sober 'hodden-grey'[8], enlivened only by the famous blue bonnet. Pikemen did not wear armour, unlike their English counterparts, partly on grounds of cost but perhaps more due to the fact that the majority of officers had trained in Continental wars where body armour was now virtually obsolete. As muskets were in short supply, the ratio of pikes to shot was often much higher than south of the border, though the Scots purchased some 31,671 muskets from European suppliers between 1639 and 1644[9]. Infantry regiments were formed in companies, though totals varied anywhere from five to a dozen and total strength rarely exceeded half a thousand.

Cavalry, formed into regiments of eight troops with a complement of, say, threescore riders plus their officers, were less expensively equipped than their English counterparts and more reliant upon the lance, a weapon discarded almost everywhere else. The horse with their sober hues, leather coats or jacks and burgonets[10] may closely have resembled their reiver ancestors and indeed, from time to time, the ranks may have been filled with a few mosstroopers[11]. When the trumpet call to battle sounded, the mounted regiment divided into two squadrons, one under the major or second in command, the other led by a senior captain.

Highlanders, of whom a number would always be present, attracted by employment in arms and the lure of spoil, would still wear their traditional plaids, though clan tartans in the nineteenth-century romantic sense were largely unknown. These hardy fighters would prefer their own weapons, broadsword and dirk, the fearsome Lochaber axe[12] and rounded targes. Few would have firearms; more would probably still carry bows as the preferred missile weapon. Stuart Reid describes these clansmen as a 'mob' but this is somewhat unfair – these were men inured to war, many were semi-professional fighting men or caterans and the authority of the clan chief was near-absolute, normally the chief and his immediate family or tacksmen[13] formed the officer cadre. The fearsome and much lauded highland charge was in all probability a creation of the Civil Wars, introduced, it is said, by the Irish paladin Alasdair MacColla.

Leven's invading force of 1640 was well equipped with cannon and he used these pieces to good effect at Newburn Ford. When he returned four year later, the train was even more formidable:

Eight brass demi-cannon (24lb shot)
One brass culverin (18lb shot)
Three brass quarter-cannon (12lb shot)
Nine iron demi-culverins (9lb shot)
Forty-eight brass demi-culverin (9lb shot)
Eight petard mortars
Eighty-eight 'frames (3lb shot)[14]

It is worth noting that, despite this great weight of ordnance, the Scots guns did little service in the field at Marston Moor and were used against the walls firstly of York and then Newcastle to bombard (i.e. fire over the walls), rather than to batter them down. The breaches in both sieges were intended to be effected by mining. There follows a list of those Scottish regiments of foot which participated in the Siege of Newcastle:

Angus Foot
Aytouns Foot
Clydedale Foot
College of Justice/Sinclairs Foot
Edinburgh Foot
Fife Foot
Galloway Foot
Glencairns Foot
Earl of Lanarks Foot
Earl of Loudouns Foot
East Lothian Regiment
Kyle & Carrick Foot
Linlithgow & Tweeddale Foot
Master of Cranstouns Foot

Mearns & Aberdeen Foot
Merse Foot
Midlothian Foot (part)
Ministers Foot
Niddries Foot
Nithsdale & Annandale Foot
Perthshire/Gask Foot (part)
Perthshire-Freelands Foot
Stirlingshire Foot
Strathearn Foot
Teviotdale Foot
Tweedale Foot
Viscount Kenmures Foot

Appendix 4

The Battlefield Trail Today

One might easily be forgiven for assuming that the squat cooling towers at Stella have obscured all traces of the battle that raged there in August 1640, but the battlefield detective may be pleasantly surprised. Despite all of the modern development and the fact the river's course has shifted, Newburn Church still stands and the present bridge crosses at the same point as one of the major fords. A useful network of riverside paths gives us access to much of the ground and an interpretation panel has been erected. The location of one of the sconces may be detected and the view from the south towards Newburn and the high ground to the north conveys a clear impression of the strength of the Scots' position and the skill with which Leslie deployed his forces and particularly his guns.

There is much useful information to be found on the UK Battlefield Trust website (www.battlefieldstrust.com/rsource/civil-war). Sentinel Hill, where Leslie located his easterly batteries was subsequently worked as a sand quarry and it was said that the bones of those interred there, together with horse skeletons were uncovered during digging, together with cannon and musket shot. It was also said that as the English reserve from Whickham withdrew, they did so in such unseemly haste there was no time to properly strike their camp which was simply burnt. A legend grew that the fire ignited a coal seam which smouldered for a whole generation! Quantities of equipment and leather water bottles were apparently found in the Coaly Well prior to its being filled in.

It is sensible to begin a perambulation in the Castle Garth, still, where not obscured by the railway, dominated by the twelfth-century keep and thirteenth-century barbican. More of the medieval traces have been uncovered in recent years and the site, allowing for the later distractions, certainly repays an inspection. Beneath the great square stone donjon lies the original Roman fort of Pons Aelius[1] (lines in the paving mark the Roman buildings) and the Black Gate forms the tip of a roughly triangular plateau. On the south side significant traces of the curtain wall and postern survive, overlooking a sharp drop down to the river. This is the key to the enceinte's position. If we can cast a powerful beam of imagination to strip away later industrial age intrusions, we can see how completely this ground dominates the crossing. It is a very strong site indeed, with contours dipping away sharply on two sides of the triangle. Only on the westwards side, facing Cathedral Buildings and the nineteenth-century townscape, is the ground level and here the defences were protected by a deep ditch.

Built in the reign of Henry III, the Black Gate was added around 1250 just north west of the original north gate with a bridge pit[2] between. At this point the town had no encircling stone walls these were also a thirteenth-century addition and the castle now lay within the circuit. Walls were needed in Northumberland for the best part of the ensuing three centuries, the Anglo-Scottish wars spluttered from 1296 to 1568[3], raid and foray, skirmish and battle provided an enduring template for the times. Despite these regular martial clarions the fabric of the castle was generally subject to decay. Those two additional stories were added to the Black Gate in the early seventeenth century; and a bastion constructed beside the keep on top of what was likely the very first construction (traces of which have survived)[4]. The ruination of the once lofty keep was only halted in the nineteenth century when the corporation acquired the site and various restorations, notably those by Dobson[5] and the Society of Antiquaries of Newcastle upon Tyne, were undertaken.

The keep is rather a late example of Norman work and is further distinguished by the survival of the fore-building, a feature not often preserved[6]. Internally, the building has one large apartment on each floor with smaller chambers and stairs set in the great thickness of the walls. The first-floor hall houses a collection of artefacts, many of them from the Civil War period, including some interesting arms and armour. More weapons from the era can be seen in Discovery Museum on Blandford Street, including some fine swords and a superlative pair of late sixteenth-century daggs. Upstairs in the keep within the King's Chamber off the Great Hall, some graffiti from the Civil War period survives, incised into the masonry. From the roof (a steep ascent but worthwhile) one has a magnificent view of the city, with the curse of the railway out of immediate sight. Looking southwards to the Gateshead side it is immediately apparent how the high ground there dominates the north bank. Again much modern development rather obscures our understanding.

Murage was first granted in 1265[7] and, as discussed previously, the line of the town wall was intact in the seventeenth century and a satisfying and perhaps surprising amount survives. The total extent of the walk is around 3 miles (5km) and begins in the Castle Garth. Descending to the Quayside through the surviving south postern, we walk westwards along Closegate – of this grand portal no trace remains but there is a commemorative plaque and floor lines marking the extent within the foyer of the Copthorne Hotel. Opposite, traces of surviving masonry remain showing the steep ascent from Whitefriar Tower. The landscaped areas within now obscure the site of the medieval Carmelite friary. If we swing right further along and make our journey up the steep incline of Hanover Street a significant stretch of surviving wall can be viewed off Orchard Street, in the car park adjoining a modern casino.

Our direction now lies past the Central Station to the junction of Westgate Road and Clayton Street. No hint of the gate still stands but by far the best preserved and most continuous stretch of wall stands along the line of Cross Street/Bath Lane and Stowell Street with the Heber and Morden Towers. Adjacent stands the thirteenth-century Blackfriars, a monastic community which survived until the Dissolution in 1539, substantial traces remain and the site now houses craft-based activities. Along the flank leading north-east a section of the ditch is exposed, giving the best and easiest understanding of the overall construction of the medieval defences. Continuing in this direction a further stretch of wall still stands behind St Andrew's Church. From here, head eastwards along the line of Blackett Street and Newbridge Street West; Pilgrim Gate stood at the junction with Pilgrim Street though again no trace remains. From the corner occupied by the Carliol Tower[8] the walls swung south east through Plummer Tower[9] down towards the Sandgate[10].

Considerable powers of imagination do need to be conjured to push away all traces of the modern bustle, nineteenth-century development overlaid with random post-war buildings, habitually of limited aesthetic appeal and, on the western flank newer, large forms of construction maintaining the same dismal cheapness and dire conformity. Visualise an altogether different city, a jumble of tall, encroaching timber-framed shops and dwellings, piled in confusion as though they had arisen by force of nature, smoking, stinking, heaving, teeming and loud. Banish all electronic noises; hear only the clangour of church bells, the calling of street vendors, the hammering and urgency of local enterprise.

Aside from Discovery Museum, there is little local or even regional commemoration, though Tyne and Wear Museums are moving impressively to fill the void. Even the field of Marston Moor, apart from the monument itself, is poorly interpreted. By far the best displays of arms and armour are to be seen in Bamburgh Castle, Leeds Armouries and Castle Museum, York. Further afield, the Wallace Collection in London has a superb range of arms from the period. An excellent reference collection is maintained by Newcastle City Libraries together with the Literary and Philosophical Society Library and the Society of Antiquaries Library in Great North Museum. For those who wish to understand the campaigns in the north better, the most accessible single volume work is Stuart Reid's *All the King's Armies*. The keep is currently and admirably maintained by the City of Newcastle upon Tyne and open to visitors, the Black Gate, in the care of the Society of Antiquaries, is not presently accessible.

In the north-east region there are a number of historic sites which have Civil War connections: Tynemouth Castle, secularised after the Dissolution, played a role in the siege and did not fall to the Scots until after the storming of Newcastle. Four years later, it was the site of a significant engagement. Morpeth Castle, which changed hands no less than five times, in 1644, survives at least in part, as does Medieval Prudhoe Castle, which held a Royalist garrison from 1642–4 and played a role in the cat and mouse game between the armies after the Scots invasion in January 1644. Warkworth Castle was fitfully garrisoned but surrendered without a shot being fired in 1644[11].

Appendix 5

The Storming of Newcastle – Poem

Ye want to hear th' story, lad!
Aa's syre ye've little need,
Ye've heard it tell'd that often
Ye could tell 't to me I'steed.
But cum sit doon, it's yit an hoor
Before wor keel's away,
And lissen hoo Newcassel fell
On that October day.

That dark October morning, tired,
Upon the walls we lay,
The styens that neet wor pillows, as
We watched th' morning grey.
An ivory man thor knew and wished,
Before th' sun went doon,
That bloody strife wad settle whe'
Should hev Newcassel toon.

For whe' but us closed in the toon
Could tell the bitter need –
Muthors hiding, white an' trembling;
Bairens crying oot for breed.
Such seits and sounds before wor eyes,
An' ringin' I' wor ears.
Myed brave the weakest o' wor hearts,
And drove away thor fears.

We knew thor mines wor ready laid,
Thor men in ranks could see;
We knew they thorty thoosin wor –
Poor fifteen hundred we.
But Marley cried, 'Yor walls are strang;
Keep heart, lads, nivvor feor;
Although they're swarming thick around,
Ne blue cap gets in heor.'

Thor canting League an' Covenant
We cannot heor abide;
That an thor Parliament we scorn –
King Charlie is wor pride…
[Here there is a break in the manuscript]
… Shieldfield Fort …
we born'd it te the grund,
an' as it born'd an' lowed amain
wor streets wor let as day.
Se bleezin' come the nineteenth in
That closed wor bitter fray.

It fund me on the aad west wall
The Tyne ran at me feet
And Whickham's bonny banks slop'd doon
The banks of Tyne te meet
An' bonny though they elwis are,
We'd eyes for nowt that day,
But how te watch wor batter'd waals
And haud the foe at bay,

For now in fury aall around
They raged wi' fearful din,
An' high above the trumpit's call
The cannon thunder'd in.
The shot was splint'ring doon the waaks,
Greet gaps wor opning wide,
An', geth'ring for the closin' spring,
They crooded ev'ry side.

Yor fethor, clicking hard ma hand,
Cries, 'Jack, at last they're heor';
Ah nivvor hard his voice agyen –
That voice that knew ne feor.
For as we stood aall trembling feel'd
The grund belaw wor feet,
Then wiv a thunder'n fearful roar,
Aall vanished frae ma seet.

They'd fired a mine, an' walls an' men,
Like dust, wor blaan away;
Whor mony fell, as liv'd te tell
The ruin of that day.
Aye, lived to find that by ma side
Yor fethor killed thor lay –
An' aad Newcassel toon, wor pride,
Was lost an' torn away.

Appendix 6

Mapping the Wars

Chorography is defined by the OED as:

> The art or practice of describing, or of delineating on a map or chart, particular regions, or districts; as distinguished from 'geography', taken as dealing with the earth in general, and (less distinctly) from 'topography' which deals with particular places or towns.

Jerome de Groot in *Chorographia Newcastle and the Royalist Identity in the Late 1640s* observes that the period of the late 1640s was a rather 'bad' place for Royalists. Established tradition and natural order in the world were topsy-turvy, the Regicides had struck a monumental blow at the foundations of accepted English society and ushered in a period of desperate uncertainty.

Long held allegiances, assumptions about the social order, have been rent asunder by the dire vicissitudes of Civil War. These are terrible and frightening times, radical sectaries like Levellers and Diggers threaten the very fabric of hierarchical society. Gray's *Chorographia* is a Royalist response; he overturns the Parliamentarian condemnation of the city as a hotbed of malignancy to portray Newcastle as a symbol of proper defiance. His printer, Stephen Bulkley, was a staunch Royalist who had employed his art diligently in the King's service. Gray was a burgess and his work is intended to validate the city's honour through its adherence. His tone is one of civic defiance, a setting straight of the record. Whatever anarchies the Parliamentary triumph may have set in train, the city of Newcastle retains its place in the Royalist firmament (not one particularly recognised by the Cavaliers during the siege it must be admitted).

Gray is punctilious in listing the city's ancient charters and the extensive involvement of successive monarchs. His work embodies a description of the city *Walls, Wards, Churches, Religious Houses, Streets, Markets, Fairs, River and Commodities; with the Suburbs.* It is very much restricted to the Urbs rather than county or region. Though he litters his account with anecdotes, de Groot sees the *Chorographia* as a distinct departure from more conventional Royalist manifestos. Gray lauds the city as a fountainhead of Royalism, whereas previous Caroline authors had tended to view urban locations as hotbeds of dissent and Parliamentary fervour. He sees this as 'the reality of loyalty'. He sees his work as a literary heritage, saving through his descriptions the essence of structures levelled by war and linking these to a Royalist pedigree, a testament to an unbroken history of loyalty to the Crown. His becomes the voice crying out against the tyranny of the times, the rule of venal oligarchs, harking back to the authors of antiquity, from Homer and Virgil to Camden.

Gray does not trouble to conceal his political bias, indeed his partisan leanings are expressed as being of the essence. His role is one of setting the record straight, of countering the malign influence of revisionist revolutionaries and, by implication, the prevailing Puritan cabal. He reverts to the tried portrayal of Newcastle as a primary bulwark against the Scots. Here, he taps into not just a local vein. The alliance between Parliament and the Scottish Estates was at best one of necessity, there was little real sympathy between the parties and, in real terms, the Scots Army, for all its paper strength, achieved little beyond the reduction of Newcastle. Leven's role at Marston Moor was less than heroic; left to the Scots, Rupert would have won the day. Here, Gray, who waxes lyrical on the subject of the barbarous Scots, a theme many Englishmen, regardless of affiliation, would have heartily endorsed.

Appendix 7

The Order to Reduce Newcastle

Appointment of Committee of Lords and Commons.

Whereas the greatest part of this Kingdom, and more especially the City of London, and most Maritime towns, are served and furnished with Coals from the town of Newcastle upon Tyne, and the adjacent parts of Northumberland, and the Bishoprick of Durham, which being now kept by Forces consisting of Papists, and other ill-affected persons under the command of the Earle of New-castle: the City of London, and all the greatest part of this Kingdom are like to suffer very deeply in the want of that commodity so absolutely necessary to the maintenance and support of life, and which is like to be of very dangerous consequence in the influence which it may have upon the necessities of the meaner sort. And whereas 'tis also very dangerous to adventure shipping within the command of the Forts there erected, as being subjected to a surprize, and like enough to be made use of against the safetie of the Kingdome, if they should make their voyage onely man'd as usually for trade; And how great use has beene made of the port of Newcastle, to the danger of the Kingdome, since it came into the hands of the said Earle is manifest to all. It is therefore hoped that there are none that will be backward to contribute their best asistance towards the reducing of that place, in the recovery whereof all men are interested, and the rather for the opportunity which is now given, if it be speedily undertaken, and effectually prosecuted. And whereas in obedience to an Order of the House of Commons the Committee of the Navy communicated their opinions in writing to the Lord Major of London by what means the said City may be furnished with coales, with desire that his Lordship would impart the same to the Aldermen of that City, or such other persons as his Lordship should thinke fit, which Writing, with the Petition and propositions of divers Citizens of London, were read at a Commoncouncell, held at Guild-hall in London, the twentieth of this moneth, where the said Court taking all the premises into their serious consideration did conceive that this great worke might be effected, if both Houses of Parliament should thinke fit to approve of these ensuing Propositions. Wherefore the Lords and Commons in Parliament assembled, upon mature deliberation had of the Propositions following, and well approving the good affections of the Citie of London to the publique service, and of all such other well-affected persons as shall subscribe and pay in any considerable summe of money according to the ensuing Propositions, for, and towards this great and necessary undertaking, doe Order and Ordaine in manner and forme following: And first the House of Commons doe consent to nominate ten of their own Members, And the Lords and Commons doe Order and Ordaine, that the Common-councell of London shall nominate a like number for the City, to be a Committee joyntly to mannage all affaires touching this adventure, and to call to their assistance in this service such of the out ports, or others, as they shall thinke fit.

Its Powers.

2. That the said Committee so to be nominated shall have power to make Sub-committees among themselves, and to give them such instructions as they shall thinke fit, being pursuant and agreeable to these Propositions, and to prepare bookes for such subscriptions, to appoint persons from time to time in all places to take the same, and to receive all such moneys as shall be subscribed, and paid in according to such subscriptions, and to return or issue out the same to such persons, and in such manner, as the said Committee, or the greater number of them shall direct.

Moneys advanced to be paid to Treasurers and employed only for reducing Newcastle.

3. That all Moneys to bee advanced upon these Propositions shall bee paid to such Treasurers as the said Committee shall appoint, and shall be onely imployed by the said Committee for the reducing of the said Town of Newcastle, and the said parts adjacent till the same be effected and to none other purpose whatsoever.

Tax on Traders in Coal, etc., to Newcastle, Sunderland, or Blith, that do not subscribe half their stock to these Propositions.

4. That they shall be accountable to such persons as shall be appointed by both Houses; that every Owner or Master, of, or in, any ship or ships, trading for Coals, Salt, or Glasse, to the towns of Newcastle, Sunderland or Blith, or to any place adjacent now under the power of the Earle of Newcastle, and not subscribing one halfe of his stock which he hath in any such Ship or ships, to these Propositions, within one moneth after these Propositions shall be agreed upon by the Lords and Commons in Parliament, shall pay to the persons to be appointed by the said Committee to receive the same, for every Chaldron of coals he shall so buy there, the summe of foure shillings, and for every weigh of Salt two shillings, and for every case of Glasse one shilling more then shall be paid by any Adventurer tha shall buy there any of the said commodities of Coals, Salt, or Glasse; The said payments to be made to the use of the Adventurers upon Accounts, and to continue till the said Adventurers shall be reimbursed, according to the ensuing Propositions, and no longer.

Tax on all persons in London, etc., that buy Newcastle coals and do not subscribe proportionably.

5. That every person within the said City of London, or ten miles thereof, or within such of the out-Ports or Cities, or dwelling upon any navigable River, or within five miles of any of them which have or shall have their Coals from any of the said towns of Newcastle, Sunderland, Blith, or places adjacent, which shall not subscribe to these Propositions within one moneth after the same shall be agreed upon by both houses of Parliament, a summe of Money at least proportionable to the Coales he annually expends in his house in the judgement of the said Committee (such as are not Subsidie-men onely excepted) shal pay

ten shillings for every chaldron of coals more then others shall pay that doe subscribe, the same payments to bee made and collected to the use of the Adventureres upon accompt, in such manner as the said Committee shall appoint, and to continue untill the said Adventurers shall be reimbursed according to the insuing Propositions, and no longer.

Punishment for fraudulently furnishing coals to nonsubscribers.

6. That if any subscriber shall use any fraudulent or indirect means to furnish any other person with coals, that shall not subscribe within the time before limited, such Subscriber shall forfeit the benefit of his own subscription, and both parties shall be liable to such further punishment as shall be inflicted by both Houses of Parliament.

None to sell Newcastle Coals in London, etc., unless he subscribe proportionably.

7. That no person shall be permitted to sell Coals in London, or any other Port or place, which is or shall be furnished with Coals from the said town of New-castle, Sunderland, Blith, and places adjacent, unlesse such as shall subscribe a sum proportionable to their trade, in the judgement of the said Committee.

Papists' and Delinquents' Estates sequestered for use of Adventurers.

8. That two parts of the estates of Papists, not Delinquents, and all the estates of such as are declared to be Delinquents, by the Ordinance of Sequestration within the County of Northumberland, the County and Bishoprick of Durham, and in the towne and county of New-castle upon Tyne, shall be forthwith sequestred, and all such moneys as shall be raised thereby, shall be also payed to the use of the said Adventurers upon accompt, untill the said Adventurers shall be reimbursed, according to the insuing Propositions, and no longer.

Duties on Coals, etc., in Newcastle, Sunderland, and Blith to be for use of Adventurers.; Committee may propound Officers for Land Service.

9. That all such Customs, Duties, and Imposts as have been usually paid, or shall be thought fit to be paid by any Ordinance of Parliament, for Coals, Salt, and Glasse, within the said Town and County of New-castle, the said town of Sunderland, Blith, and the said parts adjacent, shall be paid to the use of the said Adventurers upon accompt, as aforesaid. That the said Committee shall have power to propound all Officers for the Land service of this Designe to the Lord Generall for his approbation of them, who is hereby desired forthwith to grant Commissions to such Officers so approved of by him, according to the quality of their severall commands.

And Officers for Officers for Sea-service.

10. That the said Committee shall have power to propound all Officers for the Sea-service of this Designe to the Commissioners of the Admiralty, and the Earle of Warwick, for their approbation, and the said Earl of Warwick is desired for the present to give Commissions and Instructions to the severall Sea-Officers so approved of according to the nature of their severall Imployments.

Forces for Expedition to be disposed by Committee. Commanders.

11. That all the Forces that shall be raised by Land and Sea for this Expedition, shall be ordered and disposed by the said Committee, yet so as the said Land-Forces shall bee subject to the command and controll of the Lord Generall and the Lord Fairfax, and the Sea Forces subject to the command and controll of the Earle of Warwick, in such manner as shall most conduce to this present Expedition.

On Reduction of Newcastle, etc., all moneys lent to be repaid with interest.; Adventurers meanwhile to have 8 l. per Cent. Interest.

12. That when the said Towns of Newcastle, Sunderland, and Blith, and the parts adjacent, now under the power of the Earle of New-castle, shall be freed from that grievous oppression, and reduced under the Authority of King and Parliament, then it shall be lawfull for the said Committee to pay or cause to be paid to every Subscriber, for every twenty shillings which he shall have paid in for this service, £1 6s 8d in such manner as in the ensuing Article is exprest, and so after that rate for a greater sum: And for the further incouragement to this Designe, It is ordered and Ordained, That until the said towns of New-castle, Sunderland, Blith, and the said parts adjacent, be reduced, the Adventurers shall have Interest at 8 l. per Cent. for their principall Adventure.

Repayment to be made in order of Subscriptions.

13. That all such persons as within London, or within five miles thereof, shall subscribe and pay in a third part of the sum subscribed within ten dayes after these Propositions shall be agreed upon by both Houses of Parliament, and another third part within twenty-eight dayes after such Subscription, and the last third part within fifty six dayes after such subscription. And all such persons as in any other Port, City, or Town, shall subscribe and pay in a third part of the sum subscribed, to such persons as shall be appointed by the said Committee to receive the said Subscriptions and Moneys, within ten dayes after these Propositions shall be delivered to the Head Officers or Head Officer of such Port, City, or Town, and shall pay in the other two parts as aforesaid, shall be repaid their Moneys, together with their proceed by equall proportions: And all such persons as shall subscribe after the said space of ten dayes, and pay in their Moneys as aforesaid, shall be paid in such order as they shall subscribe.

Notes

Chapter 1

1. Welford, R., 'Newcastle Householders in 1655; Assessment of Hearth or Chimney Tax' in *Archaeologia Aeliana* 3rd Series vol. 7, pp 49–76
2. Howell, R. jnr., *Newcastle upon Tyne and the Puritan Revolution: A Study of the Civil War in the North of England* (Oxford, 1967), p. 6
3. Howell, p. 11
4. Langton, J., 'Residential Patterns in Pre-Industrial Cities' in *The Tudor and Stuart Town – a Reader in English Urban History 1530–1688* ed. J. Barry (London, 1990), p. 171
5. Those who became successful in commerce or industry often moved from city to shire; perhaps Lord Armstrong (1810–1900) whose magnificent house at Cragside near Rothbury was built on the proceeds of his Elswick Gun Works, remains the prime example
6. Langton, pp 166–206
7. PRO SP E 179/158/104 cited in Howell, p. 350
8. Gray, W., *Chorographia or a survey of Newcastle-upon-Tine* (Newcastle, 1649)
9. 'The Journal of Sir William Brereton 1635' in *North Country Diaries* ed. J.C. Hodgeson, Surtees Society 124 (1915)
10. See Trevelyan G.M., *English Social History: A Review of Six Centuries – Chaucer to Queen Victoria* (London, 1946)
11. Chamberlains' Accounts, Tyne and Wear Archives (TW 543/18)
12. See Wrightson, K., 'Continuity, Chance and Change. The Character of the Industrial Revolution in England – Elements of Identity' in *Northumberland, History and Identity* ed. R. Collis (Stroud, 2007)
13. Nef, J.U., *Rise of the British Coal Industry* (London, 1966)
14. Foster, Heralds Visitation Records, p. 39
15. From the French – 'to hear and determine'
16. Keeper of the English County Court records
17. Delaval Family Papers; Northumberland County Archives Service 1 DE & 2 DE
18. Blackett Family papers; Northumberland County Archives Service ZBK
19. *Journal of the House of Commons* cited in Howells, p. 124
20. Andrews, G., *The Acts of the High Commission Court within the Diocese of Durham* Surtees Society 34 (1858), p. 159
21. Hunter-Blair, P., *Mayors and Sheriffs of Newcastle*, pp 29–33 and *History of Durham*, Surtees Society 2, p. 269
22. Welford R., *Men of Mark twixt Tyne and Tweed* (London and Newcastle, 1985)
23. Foster, S., *The Long Argument; English Puritanism and the Shaping of New England Culture 1570–1700*
24. Cookson, G., *Coal Trade on the Wear before 1800*
25. Gray, *Chorographia*

26. Quoted in Mabbit, J., *Archaeology, Revolution and the end of the Medieval English Town; Fortification and Discourse in Seventeenth Century Newcastle upon Tyne* (unpublished paper), p. 5
27. *Ibid.*, p. 6
28. *Ibid.*, p. 7
29. Quoted in Mabbit, p. 8
30. *Ibid*, p. 9
31. Mackenzie, E., *A Descriptive and Historical Account of the Town and County of Newcastle upon Tyne Including the Borough of Gateshead* (Newcastle 1827) vol. I, p. 106
32. Quoted in Mackenzie, p. 106
33. *Ibid.*
34. *Ibid.*, p. 107
35. *Ibid.*, p. 109
36. *Ibid.*, p. 111
37. A gilded ball which decorated the meeting hall was said to have been a ball shot by the Scots during the siege
38. This was, in the medieval period, known as the Berwick Gate, through it passed the Bishop of Durham's reinforcement following Hotspur on the road to defeat at Otterburn in August, 1388, Mackenzie, p. 111
39. Used by the Weaver's Guild after 1682
40. This was not paved over until 1696
41. Middlebrook, S., *Newcastle upon Tyne, its Growth and Achievement* (Newcastle upon Tyne, 1950), p. 82

Chapter 2

1. Clarendon, XI, p. 239, quoted in Haythornthwaite. P., *The English Civil War 1642–1651* (London, 1994), p. 10
2. Clarendon, *ibid.* p. 240, quoted in Haythornthwaite, *ibid.*
3. Soteriological beliefs within Protestantism following the teaching of the Dutch reformer Jacobus Arminius (1560–1609)
4. Introduced first in 1563 these were a set of definitions which clearly differentiated between Anglican and Roman Catholic practice – the mantra of the reformed Church
5. These were (1) condemnation of religious innovation (2) condemnation of illegal taxes, particularly those of tonnage and poundage (3) a further condemnation of those traders who paid such illegal taxes, making them complicit in the wrongdoing!
6. Originally a medieval legitimate imposition intended to oblige coastal towns and ports to meet the cost of naval precautions in time of war only
7. Puritans were wedded, *inter alia*, to the notion of predestination
8. These included Sir John Eliot who had been a particularly inflamed critic of Buckingham, his death in the Tower further fuelled prevailing outrage
9. William Laud (1633–1645) was an ambitious and capable prelate of modest antecedents. His tenure from 1633 was marked by opposition to the Puritans exemplified by a stubborn upholding of the apostolic succession
10. Robert II and Robert II were viewed (unfairly perhaps) as undistinguished; the Anglophobe James II was murdered, his son James II, after a savage internecine battle against the Black Douglas, died when one of his own guns exploded at the Siege of Roxburgh; James III was murdered after his defeat at Sauchieburn and James IV died in the wrack of catastrophe at Flodden. James V suffered a more humiliating if less bloody reverse than his father and died, it is said, of shame; his daughter Mary after a long incarceration went to the block and James VI left Scotland without a backward glance
11. *Laud's Liturgy*, as the *Book of Canons* is forever labelled, would have replaced the established *Book of Common Order*. Laud's imposition was in fact drafted by Scottish bishops and represented a less radical step than the outright imposition of the *English Prayer Book*; this did nothing for its overall popularity

12. The Covenant was a carefully drafted response, based broadly on the *Negative Confession* of 1581. It was a document which embodied a revolutionary principle in that no innovations in church and state were to proceed without the sanction of a free parliament and General Assembly – as such it was a direct refutation of the Royal Prerogative

13. The Covenant was essentially a Lowland ideal, the conservative and mainly Catholic clans of the Western Highlands and Islands did not participate, with the notable exception of Archibald Campbell an enthusiastic supporter

14. Entered into in June 1639 – a settlement that settled nothing

15. Thomas Wentworth, 1st Earl of Strafford – steadfastly loyal to the King and a leading figure in his administration, he acted as Lord Deputy of Ireland from 1632–39, where he was noted for uncompromising harshness. The final reward for his adherence was impeachment and execution

16. Sadler, D.J., *Battle for Northumbria* (Newcastle, 1988), p. 137

17. Mackenzie, vol. I, p. 25

18. This was to be no casual raid; everything that was requisitioned was to be paid for

19. Jacob Astley, 1st Baron Astley of Reading (1579–1652) – distinguished Royalist commander during the First Civil War

20. Mackenzie, p. 25

21. The river remained silted until the emergence of Armstrong's Elswick Works in the nineteenth century

22. Mackenzie, p. 25

23. Leather guns were a Swedish invention intended to create a lighter more easily portable form of cannon constructed from a thin copper tube, tied with rope and bound in leather, ingenious but not particularly successful, generally wore out after no more than a dozen rounds

24. Mackenzie, p. 25

25. *Ibid.*

26. *Ibid.*

27. *Ibid.*

28. Brand, J., *The History and Antiquities of the Town and County of Newcastle upon Tyne* (London, 1789) vol. II, p. 284

29. Mackenzie, p. 26

30. *Ibid.*

31. *Ibid.*

32. *Ibid.*

33. *Ibid.*

Chapter 3

1. An obvious example would be Sir Edmund Verney, Knight Marshal of the Household, killed defending the King's colours at Edgehill

2. The Triennial of Dissolution Act, passed on 15 February 1641, provided that Parliament should meet for at least a fifty-day session in every three years

3. What became the Irish Confederate Wars began in earnest in 1641 as an attempt by Catholic Gentry to expel the encroaching Protestants and rapidly became a war between Catholics and Protestants in Ireland

4. These were: John Pym, John Hampden, Denzil Holles, Arthur Haselrig and William Strode

5. The Militia were effectively a Home Guard formation, a hangover from medieval practice

6. Robin Devereux, Earl of Essex (1591–1646), a popular if inconsistent general, if he did not win the Civil War for Parliament, it could at least be said he avoided losing it

7. Sir John Hotham was governor of Hull; his loyalties were by no means fixed

8. Rupert of the Rhine (1619–1682) was a younger son of Frederick V, Elector Palatine and his wife Elizabeth, a daughter of James I of England

9. 1618–48; ended by the treaty of Westphalia, one of the most destructive of all European Wars

10. Haythornthwaite, p. 58

11. Sir Ralph, Lord Hopton (1596–1651), outstanding commander of Royalist forces in the west

12. Langton, p. 171
13. Howell, p. 44
14. *Ibid.*, p. 47
15. Newcastle upon Tyne Record Series vols. 1 & 3; Extracts from the Newcastle Council Minute Book 1639–1656 ed. M.H. Dodds (Newcastle, 1920); *The Register of Freemen of Newcastle upon Tyne from the Corporation, Guild and Admission Books chiefly of the Seventeenth Century* ed. M.H. Dodds (Newcastle 1923)
16. Records of the Merchant Adventurers of Newcastle Upon Tyne (1895), p. 199-205
17. Langton, p. 171
18. Howell, citing State Papers held in the Public Record Office, p. 57
19. Newton, D., 'Doleful Dumpes; Northumberland and the Borders 1580–1625' in *Northumberland; History and Identity*, ed. R. Collis (Stroud, 2007)
20. Calendar of State Papers cited in Howell, p. 88
21. Mackenzie, pp 26–7
22. *Ibid.*
23. *Ibid.*
24. *Ibid.*
25. *Ibid.*
26. C.S. Terry MA in *Achaeologia Aeliana New Series* vol. XXI, p. 84
27. *Ibid.*, p. 85
28. A copy of the full text is set out in Terry p. 91 *et seq.*
29. Rushworth, *Historical Collection of Private Passages of State 1629–1638* vol. ii, p. 178
30. Terry, p. 96
31. *Ibid.*
32. *Ibid.*
33. *Ibid.*, p. 97
34. *Ibid.*
35. *Ibid.*, p. 99
36. *Ibid.*
37. *Ibid.*, p. 100
38. *Ibid.*, p. 101
39. *Ibid.*, p. 102
40. *Archaeologia Aeliana* vol. vi, p. 226
41. *His Majesties Passing Through the Scots Army Pamphlet* 1641
42. *Ibid.*
43. 'Redshanks' was a name derived from Scots mercenaries who fought in the Civil Wars in Ireland
44. Terry, p. 105
45. *Ibid.*, p. 106

Chapter 4

1. Hartlepool, at this time, was also in Royalist hands but the harbour was of insufficient size
2. Reid, S., *All the King's Armies – a Military History of the English Civil War 1642–1651* (Staplehurst, 1998), p. 69
3. *Ibid.*
4. Gardiner, S. R., *History of the Great Civil War Vol. 1* (London, 1987) p. 87
5. *Ibid.*
6. Grid reference SE 215289
7. UK Battlefields Trust Resource Centre
8. Sir John Hotham, the elder (1645) was a former Sheriff of Yorkshire and had married five times. His son John (1610–45) was the eldest child of his first wife, the son was executed on 1 January 1645, followed by his father a day later
9. Reid, p. 79
10. *Ibid.* p. 81 (n)

11. *Ibid.* p. 85 (n)
12. Grid reference SU 019651
13. Reid, p. 89
14. *Ibid.*
15. *Ibid.*, p. 90
16. *Ibid.*
17. *Ibid.*, p. 91
18. Grid reference TF 317684
19. Reid, p. 95
20. *Ibid.*
21. Grid reference SJ 635536
22. UK Battlefields Trust Resource Centre
23. Reid, p. 99
24. *Ibid.*, p. 104
25. *Ibid.*

Chapter 5

1. An Ordinance with Severall Propositions 1643 (Richardson Reprints)
2. Terry, *op cit.*, p. 149
3. A Continuation of Certain Special and Remarkable Passages no. 2 3–10 January 1644
4. Terry, p. 150
5. *Ibid.*, pp 150–1
6. *Ibid.*, p. 151
7. Copies of Letters from Francis Anderson & Others (Richardson Reprints)
8. Terry, p. 152
9. Reid, *op. cit.*, pp 108–109
10. Terry, p. 154
11. *Ibid.*, p. 155
12. Warburton, E., *Memoirs of Prince Rupert and the Cavaliers* vol. ii, p. 368
13. Terry, p. 156
14. Firth (ed.) *Life of William Cavendish, Duke of Newcastle by Margaret Duchess of Newcastle*, p. 347
15. Portland MSS, Hist. MSS Comm. P. 1 app. P. 169
16. The Signatories were: John Morley, Nicholas Cole, Lionel Maddison, Mark Milbanke, Francis Anderson, Ralph Cocke, Robert Shafttoe, Ralph Grey, Henry Newcastle, Thomas Lydell, Alexander Davison, Francis Bowes, Henry Maddison, Leonard Carr, Cuthbert Carr, John Emerson & Charles Clarke, see Terry, p. 158
17. *A True Relation of the late Proceedings of the Scottish Army* (Early English Books 1641–1700, Thomason Collection British Library)
18. *True Relation* etc
19. Quoted in Terry, p. 160
20. Quoted in Terry, p. 161
21. *Memoirs of Prince Rupert* etc vol. ii, p. 381
22. *Life of Newcastle* etc, p. 65
23. Terry, p. 162
24. *Ibid.*, p. 163
25. *True Relation* etc
26. *Ibid.*
27. *Ibid*
28. Reid, p. 113
29. *True Relation* etc
30. *Ibid.*
31. Richardson Reprints
32. Terry, p. 169
33. *Archaeologia Aeliana* vol. I, p. 213

34. Terry, p. 170
35. Reid, p. 115
36. *Ibid.*
37. *Mercurius Aulicus* 30 March 1644
38. Reid, p. 116
39. *Ibid.*
40. *Ibid.*
41. *Ibid.*
42. Terry, p. 174
43. Quoted in Terry, p. 175
44. Terry, p. 176
45. Note, Terry, p. 177
46. Terry, p. 177; Reid, p. 118
47. Quoted in Terry, pp 177–8

Chapter 6

1. Fawer, *The Siege and Story of Newcastle* (1889), p. 29
2. Rushworth, vol. v, p. 646
3. Terry, p. 181
4. Montrose was about to embark upon his remarkably if very temporarily successful campaign in Scotland, dubbed the Year of Miracles
5. Terry, p. 182
6. *Ibid.*, p. 183
7. *Ibid.*
8. Lithgow, W., *An Experimentall and Exact Relation upon that famous and renowned siege of Newcastle etc* (Edinburgh, 1645)
9. Lithgow, *Exact Relation* etc.
10. Terry, p. 187n.
11. *Ibid.*
12. *Lithgow, Exact Relation* etc
13. *Archaeologia Aeliana* vol. xv, p. 233
14. Reproduced in full in Terry, p. 189
15. Terry, p. 190
16. *Ibid.*, p. 191
17. Fawer, p. 29
18. *Diary of Mr Robert Douglas when with the Scots Army in England* 1644 (Edinburgh, 1833)
19. Quoted in Terry, p. 193
20. Alasdair MacColla commanded Montrose's Irish Brigade, a formidable warrior credited with inventing or refining the highland charge as a battle winning tactic in Ireland and Scotland
21. Fawer, p. 25
22. Reproduced in Terry, pp 194–5
23. Terry, p. 196
24. *Wisharts' Memories of Montrose* ed. Murdoch & Simpson (Edinburgh 1893), p. xxi
25. Terry, p. 198
26. Quoted in Terry, p. 199
27. *A Particular Relation* etc
28. Terry, p. 205
29. *Ibid.*, p. 206
30. *Ibid.*, pp 208–9
31. *Ibid.*, p. 210

Chapter 7

1. Brand states the fort was 67 yards by 67 yards with the bastion 20 yards square, vol. I, p. 442n
2. Lithgow
3. Terry, p. 213
4. 15 August 1645, a decisive Royalist victory
5. Terry, p. 213
6. *Ibid.*
7. *Ibid.*, p.p. 214–215
8. *Ibid.*, p. 216
9. Lithgow
10. Terry, p.p. 217–218
11. *Ibid.*, p. 219
12. Lithgow
13. Quoted in Terry, p. 221
14. *A Particular Relation* etc
15. *Ibid.*
16. The vicar of St Nicholas' – died 1649
17. *A Particular Relation* etc
18. Contemporary pamphlet: *The Taking of Newcastle, or Newes from the Armie Edinburgh*, 1644, the Society of Antiquaries of Newcastle Upon Tyne
19. Quoted in Terry, p. 226
20. Lithgow
21. *Ibid.*
22. *Ibid.*
23. *A Particular Relation* etc
24. Lithgow gives the numbers who surrendered from the Castle as seventy-two, others state improbably higher numbers. The plague in Tynemouth Castle was said to have claimed eight lives with many more sick – see Terry, p. 232 notes
25. *A Particular Relation* etc
26. Terry, p. 233

Chapter 8

1. De Groot, J., *Chorographia, Newcastle and Royalist Identity in the Late 1640s*
2. Terry, p. 235
3. *Ibid.*
4. *Ibid.*
5. *Ibid.*, p. 237
6. *Ibid.*
7. See Terry, pp 238–9 for full lists
8. NCA Chamberlain's Accounts 1642–1645 Tyne and Wear Archives (TW 543/27)
9. *Ibid.*
10. *Ibid.*
11. Lithglow
12. *ibid.*
13. Trinity House MSS Records
14. Terry, p. 243
15. *Ibid.*
16. *Ibid.*, p. 244
17. *Ibid.*
18. *Ibid.*, p. 248
19. Dodds (ed), *Newcastle Upon Tyne Record Scenes*
20. Chaldron = Cauldron, never exactly defined and varying according to locality; the Newcastle measure is 2,000lb or 910kg; the weight tended to increase as the tax element grew, by 1678

the measure was 52½ cwt, see Ashworth, W. & M. Pegg, *History of the British Coal Industry* (Oxford, 1986), p. p. 559–60

21. Terry, p. 253
22. Cal. State Papers (Dom) 1644
23. The 'Lobsters' were so called as they wore full cuirassier harness, then largely obsolescent, their performance at Roundway ('Runaway') Down was less than inspirational
24. Mackenzie, p. 43n.
25. Middlebrook, p. 77
26. 'Favver', *The Siege and Storming of Newcastle* (Newcastle upon Tyne, 1889)

Appendix 1

1. The dog-lock was an early form of flint gun much in use during the period, the cock or striking arm was restrained by an external catch affixed to the lock-plate
2. 'Apostles' were so names as they were twelve in number and made of wood for obvious reasons. It may also be the operator required the assistance of the divine so hazardous was his undertaking!
3. Pistols of the period have a large steel or brass butt plate, this was not ornamental, it protected the grip from splitting but also meant the discharged weapon (there usually being little leisure to reload) could be employed in its more basic guise of a handy bludgeon.
4. A light ambidextrous blade, handy for cut or thrust and popular in the Netherlands, Germany and Scandinavia
5. Turnham Green, where the cavaliers were, in effect, faced down by the London Trained Bands
6. Haythornthwaite, pp 24– 45
7. *Ibid.*, pp 45–52

Appendix 2

1. *Ibid.* pp 53–5 and Osprey 'Vanguard' Series no 108 *English Civil War Artillery 1642–1651*
2. 'Roaring Meg' can still be seen in Hereford, see Haythornthwaite, p. 54 and the Royal Armouries at Leeds have some very fine examples
3. Including the ordinary sort of women Willis, J.W., *Diary of Henry Townshend of Elmley* Lovett ed. J. Bund (Worcester, 1916) and quoted in Haythornthwaite, p. 55
4. When the Marquis of Winchester's garrison at Basing House was finally overcome by storming in October 1645 the Roundheads enacted a number of atrocities against civilian refugees and the savage Colonel Harrison personally murdered the actor Robbins who had lampooned him, see Wedgwood, The King's War p.p. 495–6
5. Refer to Gaunt, P., *The Cromwellian Gazetteer* (Stroud, 1987)
6. The 'Eighty Years War' (1568–1648)
7. Young, P., & W. Emberton, *Sieges of the Great Civil War* (London, 1978), p. 2
8. Roundhead Colonel Thomas Rainsborough, a great friend to the Levellers, was killed in a sally by the defenders of Pontefract in October 1648, though there is suspicion this was in fact an assassination orchestrated by Cromwell
9. Young & Embleton, *op. cit.*, p. 3
10. Quoted in Young & Embleton., p. 7
11. *Ibid.* p. 3

Appendix 3

1. The ancient provision for Wappinschaws or musters was long established in Scotland
2. The Scottish Estates comprised three principal classes of representatives: the Magnates, the Kirk and the Royal Burghs
3. Reid, *op. cit.*, p. 6
4. The exchange rate was twelve pounds Scots to one pound English – men generally provided their own war gear and the shortfall only was made up from the public purse
5. 'Fencibles' were those men defensively arrayed, i.e. capable of bearing arms

6. Reid, p. 7

7. *Ibid.*

8. Haythornthwaite, *op. cit.* p. 134

9. Reid, p. 15

10. A burgonet is a form of combed horseman's helmet with a projecting brim and hinged cheek pieces. Tyne and Wear Museums have some fine examples in their collections; in one case the comb has suffered a hefty sword blow which has left a very marked incision – nonetheless the wearer would have been safe or relatively so!

11. 'Mosstroopers' were 'broken men' or outlaws who had infested that swathe of the borders known as the 'Debateable Land'

12. The Lochaber axe and its borderer equivalent the Jeddart Staff was a formidable staff weapon intended to cleave, not entirely unlike the English bill and finished with a handy hook – these were used as late as the Forty Five; Colonel Gardiner was fatally felled by a Lochaber at Prestonpans in 1745

13. Tacksman comes from the Scottish 'tack' for lease, a tenant of the chief

14. Reid, p. 26

Appendix 4

1. Those buildings outlined comprise the west section of the HQ building and a fragment of the garrison commander's accommodation, see Pevsner, N & I. Richmond, Northumberland in the 'Buildings of England' series (London, 1992 edn.), p. 435

2. Pevsner, p. 436

3. The treaty of Berwick marked the beginning of the path which led to the Union of the Crowns in 1603 though the borders remained wild and lawless in the interim

4. Traces of this can be viewed beneath the Railway Viaduct; Pevsner, p. 436

5. The Corporation acquired the Keep in 1809, thought Dobson's refurbishments date from 1847; Pevsner, p. 436

6. The design of the forebuilding is unique aside from that surviving at Dover; Pevsner, p. 437

7. Pevsner, pp 439–40

8. Demolished in the nineteenth century when the old Central Library was built; Pevsner, p. 441

9. This was extensively re-modelled by the Company of Masons as a meeting hall in 1740 and is consequently much altered; Pevsner, p. 440

10. No trace of this or of the continuation along the quayside survives

Select Bibliography

Primary Sources

A Continuance of Certain Special and Remarkable Passages No. 2, 3–10 January 1644

A History of Northumberland issued under the direction of the Northumberland county history committee, vol. ix

An Ordinance with Severall Propositions 1643 (Richardson, Reprints)

Andrews, G., *Acts of the High Commission Court within the Diocese of Durham Surtees Society* vol. 34 (1858)

Blackett Family Records (NCRO, ZBK)

Chamberlain's accounts, Tyne & Wear Archives, TW 543/18

Craster, H.E., *The Parochial Chapelries of Earsdon and Horton* (Newcastle Upon Tyne, Andrew Reid & Co., 1909)

Como, D.R., 'Women, Prophecy, and Authority in Early Stuart Puritanism' *The Huntington Library Quarterly,* Vol. 61, No. 2 (1998), pp 203–222), Published by: University of California Press

Copies of Letters from Francis Anderson and Others (Richardson Reprints)

Delaval Family Records (NCRO, 1DE & 2DE)

'Favver' *The Siege and Storming of Newcastle* (Newcastle upon Tyne, 1889)

Fenwick, Colonel John, *Christ ruling in midst of his enemies; or, Some first fruits of the Churches deliverance, budding forth out of the crosse and sufferings,* [microform] *and some remarkable deliverances of a twentie yeeres sufferer, and now a souldier of Jesus Christ; together, with Secretarie Windebanks letters to Sr. Jacob Ashley and the Maior of Newcastle, through which the violent prosecutions of the common adversaries to exile and banishment, are very transparent. Wherein also the reader shall find in severall passages, publike and particular, some notable encouragements to wade through difficulties for the advancing of the great designe of Christ, for setting up of His kingdome, and the ruine of Antichrist* (printed for Benjamin Allen in Pope's-head Alley, 1643)

Diary of Mr Robert Douglas when with the Scots Army in England (Edinburgh, 1833)

Gray, William *Chorographia or a survey of Newcastle upon Tine* (Newcastle: Printed by S.B, 1649)

Groot, Jerome de 'Chorographia: Newcastle and Royalist Identity in the late 1640s' in *The Seventeenth Century* vol. viii issue 1 (Manchester University)

His Majesties Passing Through the Scots Army (pamphlet, 1644)

Lithgow, William, *A True experimental and Exact Relation upon that Famous and Renowned Siege of Newcastle* (Edinburgh: Printed by Robert Bryson, 1645)

NCA Chamberlain's Accounts, 1642–5, Tyne & Wear Archives, TW 543/27

Newcastle upon Tyne Record Series vol. 1 Extracts from the Newcastle Council Minute Book 1639–1656 ed. M.H. Dodds (Newcastle Upon Tyne: Northumberland Press, 1920)

Newcastle upon Tyne Record Series vol. 3 The Register of Freemen of Newcastle upon Tyne from the Corporation, Guild and Admission Books chiefly of the Seventeenth Century, M H Dodds (ed), Newcastle upon Tyne, 1923

Pedigrees Recorded at the Herald's Visitations of the County of Northumberland [1615 and 1666]. R St George. Newcastle Upon Tyne: Browne and Browne, 1891

Pedigrees recorded at the heralds' visitations of the counties of Cumberland and Westmorland: made by Richard St George, Norry, King of arms in 1615, and by William Dugdale, Norry, King of arms in 1666 ([1891?])

Raine, J., A letter from the Corporation of Newcastle upon Tyne to the Mayor and Aldermen of Berwick *Archaeologia Aeliana* (1.2 Press, April 2003)

St George, R. & George W. Marshall (ed) *The Visitation of Northumberland in 1615* (London, 1878)

The Journal of Sir William Brererton 1635 in *North Country Diaries*, J.C. Hodgeson ed. (Surtees Society, 124, 1915)

The Taking of Newcastle or Newes from the Army (Edinburgh, 1644)

Websites

http://www.archive.org/details/pedigreesrecordeoosainrich

http://www.archive.org/stream/historyofnorthum09nort/historyofnorthum09nort_djvu.txt

http://www.jstor.org/stable/3817798

http://www.manchesteruniversitypress.co.uk/uploads/docs/180061.pdf

Secondary Sources

Ashley, M., *The English Civil War* (London, 1978)

Ashworth, N. & M. Pegg, *History of the British Coal Industry* (Oxford, 1986)

Barriffe, W., *Militaries Discipline; or the Young Artilleryman* 6th edn (1661)

Bourne, H., *The History of Newcastle upon Tyne; or the Ancient and Present State of that Town* (Newcastle upon Tyne, 1736)

Brand, J., *The History and Antiquities of the Town and County of Newcastle upon Tyne* (London, 1789)

Burne, A.H., & P. Young, *The Great Civil War 1642–1646* (London, 1959)

Clarendon, Edward Hyde, *Earl of History of the Rebellion and Civil Wars in England* ed. W.D. Macray (Oxford, 1888)

Cooke, D., *The Forgotten Battle; The Battle of Adwalton Moor* (Heckmondwike, 1996)

Firth, C.H., *Cromwell's Army* 3rd edn (London, 1921)

Firth, C.H., ed. *Life of William Cavendish, Duke of Newcastle by Margaret, Duchess of Newcastle*

Forster, S., *The Long Argument: English Puritanism and the Shaping of New England Culture 1570–1700* (London, 1991)

Furgol, E., *A Regimental History of the Covenanting Armies* (Edinburgh, 1990)

Gardiner, S.R., *History of the Great Civil War 1642–1649* (London, 1886–91)

Gaunt, P., *The Cromwellian Gazeteer* (Stroud, 1987)

Haythornthwaite, P., *The English Civil War 1642–1651* (London, 1994)

Howell, R., *Newcastle upon Tyne and the Puritan Revolution: A Study of the Civil War in North England* (Oxford, 1967)

Hunter-Blair, P., *Mayors and Sheriffs of Newcastle*

Kishlanskey, M.A., *The Rise of the New Model Army* (Cambridge, 1979)

Langton, J., 'Residential Patterns in pre Industrial Cities Some Case Studies from Seventeenth Century Britain' in *The Tudor and Stuart Town: A Reader in English Urban History 1530–1688* ed. J. Barry (London, 1990)

Lawson, C.C.P., *History of the Uniforms of the British Army* vol. 1 (London, 1940)

Mabbit, J., *Archaeology, Revolution and the End of the Medieval English Town: Fortification and Discourse in Seventeenth Century Newcastle upon Tyne*

Mackenzie, E., *A Descriptive and Historical Account of the Town and County of Newcastle upon Tyne* (Newcastle upon Tyne, 1827)

Middlebrook, S., *Newcastle upon Tyne its Growth and Achievement* (Newcastle upon Tyne 1950)

Morrah, P., *Prince Rupert of the Rhine* (London, 1976)

Nef, J.U., *The Rise of the British Coal Industry* (London, 1932)

Newcastle upon Tyne Records Series, vols 1 & 3

Newton, D., 'Doleful Dumpes: Northumberland and the Borders 1580–1625' in *Northumberland, History and Identity* ed. R. Collis (Stroud, 2007)

Osprey, *New Vanguard* 108, *English Civil War Artillery 1642–1651*

Campaign 119, *Marston Moor 1644*

    Elite 25, Soldiers of the English Civil War (1) Infantry

    Elite 27, Soldiers of the English Civil War (2) Cavalry

    Fortress 9, English Civil War Fortifications 1642–1651

    Essential Histories 58, The English Civil Wars 1642–1651

    Men-at-Arms 14, The English Civil War Armies

    Men-at-Arms 331, Scots Armies of the English Civil Wars

Potter, R., & G.A. Embleton, *The English Civil War 1642–1651* (London, 1973)

Reid, S., *All the King's Armies – A Military History of the English Civil War 1642–1651* (Staplehurst, 1998)

Roots, I., *The Great Rebellion* (London, 1966)

Rushworth's *Historical Collection of Private Passages of State 1629–1638*, vol. ii

Sadler D.J., *Battle for Northumbria* (Newcastle, 1988)

Terry, C.S., *The Life and Campaigns of Alexander Leslie* (London, 1899)

The Army of the Covenant (two vols. Scottish History Society, 1917

'The Scottish Campaign in Northumberland and Durham Between January and June 1644' in *Archaeolgia Aeliana New Series* vol. xxi (1899)

The Siege of Newcastle by the Scots in 1644 (Archaeolgia)

The Register of Freeman of Newcastle upon Tyne from the Corporation Guild and Admission, Chiefly of the Seventeenth Century ed. M.H. Dodds (1923)

Trevelyan, G.M., *English Social History a Review of Six Centuries – Chaucer to Queen Victoria* (London, 1946)

Tucker, J., & L.S. Winstock ed., *The English Civil War; A Military Handbook* (London, 1972)

Warburton, E., *Memoirs of Prince Rupert and the Cavaliers*

Wedgewod, C.V., *The King's Peace* (London, 1955)

The King's War (London, 1958)

The Trial of Charles I (London, 1964)

Welford, R., 'Newcastle Householders in 1665; Assessment of Hearth or Chimney Tax' in *Archaeologia Aeliana*, Third Series vol. 7 (Newcastle, 1911)

Men of Mark twixt Tyne and Tweed (London and Newcastle, 1985)

Wenham, P., *The Great and Close Siege of York, 1644* (Kineton, 1970)

Wilson, C.A., *Food and Drink in Britain* (London, 1976)

Woolrych, A., *Battles of the English Civil War* (London, 1961)

Wrightson, K., 'Continuity, Chance and Change; the Character of the Industrial Revolution in England: Elements of Identity; the Remaking of the North East' in *Northumberland, History and Identity* ed. R. Collis (Stroud, 2007)

Young, Brigadier Peter, *Civil War England* (London, 1981)

Marston Moor 1644 (Kineton, 1970)

The English Civil War Armies (London, 1973)

With W. Emberton, *Sieges of the Great Civil War* (London, 1978)

Index